CULTURED

The Leader's Guide To Fostering A Healthy

Business Culture

William W. Walker

Table of Contents

Introduction

In today's business environment, characterized by its rapid evolution and intense competitiveness, the strategic nurturing of corporate culture stands as a linchpin for achieving organizational excellence. This book embarks on a comprehensive exploration of how companies can navigate the complexities of the modern market by fostering a culture that not only withstands challenges but thrives amidst them. It delves into the essence of what makes a corporate culture resilient and positive, arguing that such a culture is not a luxury but a necessity for organizations aiming for enduring success and relevance.

The journey to cultivating a vibrant corporate culture demands an all-encompassing approach, touching upon several critical facets of organizational life. Leadership development is highlighted as the cornerstone of this process, emphasizing the role of visionary leaders in shaping a culture that aligns with the organization's values and aspirations. The importance of open communication is explored, presenting it as the bloodstream of corporate culture that ensures ideas, concerns, and innovations freely circulate throughout the organization.

Recognition and reward systems are dissected to uncover their impact on motivating employees and reinforcing the behaviors that contribute to the organization's goals. The narrative further extends into the realms of continuous learning and employee empowerment, showcasing how these elements contribute to a culture of engagement, adaptability, and innovation. Additionally, the text tackles the complexities of strategic change management, illustrating how adept navigation of change is integral to maintaining cultural coherence and organizational agility.

This book posits that investing in these key areas lays a solid foundation for building an organizational culture that excels in multiple dimensions. It enhances employee satisfaction by creating a work environment that values and nurtures its workforce. Operational efficiency is boosted by aligning individual efforts with the organization's strategic objectives, streamlining processes, and eliminating wasteful practices. Innovation is fostered in a culture that encourages risk-taking, values diverse perspectives, and supports experimentation.

Moreover, by focusing on these strategic investments, organizations can carve out a competitive edge for themselves in the marketplace, ensuring their long-term prosperity. The text underscores the necessity of a unified effort and steadfast commitment at all levels of the organization, guided by a clear and compelling vision, to cultivate such a culture.

The overarching message of this book is that robust corporate cultures are more than just sustainable environments; they are dynamic ecosystems that drive organizations toward a legacy of success. These cultures are instrumental in defining the organization's identity, shaping its path to achieving lasting significance, and ensuring resilience in the face of the ever-shifting business landscape. Through the insights and strategies outlined in the following chapters, readers will gain a deeper understanding of how to build and nurture a corporate culture that not only survives but thrives, setting the stage for a legacy of success and sustainability.

Every business operates as a unique entity, pulsating with its own life force and distinctive characteristics. This book is not crafted as a linear, step-by-step manual; instead, it is designed to immerse you in the foundational concepts that constitute a thriving business culture. My aim is to equip you with the knowledge and insights necessary to identify the areas within your organization that may benefit from refinement or enhancement. By understanding the principles of a healthy business culture, you are empowered to tailor and apply these concepts in ways that best suit the unique needs and aspirations of your business. This approach encourages a proactive and creative engagement with the material, enabling you to cultivate a corporate environment that not only aligns with your strategic objectives but also fosters a sense of purpose and engagement among your employees.

Chapter 1: Culture

The concept of culture, while seemingly straightforward, has been the subject of extensive exploration and multiple definitions since its introduction in the mid-nineteenth century. This simple seven-letter word encompasses a complex array of components that extend far beyond its surface understanding. The introduction of culture as a pivotal business concept occurred in the 1950s, thanks to Elliott Jaques's seminal work, "The Changing Culture of a Factory." This publication detailed a comprehensive multi-year study that examined the intricate correlation between social and psychological forces, group morale, and productivity within a factory environment. Since then, the concept of culture has not only become ingrained in the business lexicon but has also emerged as a central focus in organizational development and strategy.

In contemporary discourse, culture dominates conversations about company building across various sectors. Organizations strive to emulate the cultural attributes of successful entities, proudly promote their unique cultural identity among peers, and even establish dedicated departments to cultivate and maintain their cultural ethos. The prominence of culture in discussions related to recruitment, retention, productivity, and

1

efficiency is undeniable, with it often being the focal point of TED talks and other influential platforms. However, the frequent invocation of the term has led to concerns about its dilution and the potential loss of its substantive meaning. If we struggle to define culture precisely, the question arises: how can we develop and leverage it effectively to benefit our organizations?

Historically, culture has been defined through various lenses. Edward Burnett Tylor, in his 1871 work "Primitive Culture," offered a comprehensive definition of culture as "that complex whole which includes knowledge, belief, art, morals, law, custom, and any other capabilities and habits acquired by man as a member of society." This definition, emerging during a period of burgeoning interest and development in the field of Anthropology, stood as the prevailing interpretation for the subsequent fifty years. In modern times, Merriam-Webster provides a definition of culture that captures its essence in the general sense as "the characteristic features of everyday existence shared by people in a place or time." However, for business applications, a more fitting definition is perhaps the dictionary's subsequent entry: "The set of shared attitudes, values, goals, and practices that characterizes an institution or organization."

While these definitions offer valuable insights into the multifaceted nature of culture, they also prompt further inquiry into whether they fully encapsulate the entirety of what culture represents. The exploration of culture, particularly within the context of business, reveals a dynamic and evolving concept that plays a critical role in shaping organizational identity, guiding behavior, and influencing outcomes. As we delve deeper into understanding culture's implications for businesses, it becomes clear that fostering a positive and cohesive culture is essential for long-term success and sustainability. This endeavor requires thoughtful consideration, strategic planning, and ongoing commitment at all levels of the organization to ensure that culture serves as a powerful driver of innovation, engagement, and competitive advantage.

Abstraction

The concept of culture, at its core, involves abstraction—the capacity to imbue ideas, feelings, or events with meanings that transcend the immediate sensory experiences of sight, sound, touch, taste, and smell. This abstraction is vividly illustrated in the diverse ways cultures have historically approached and honored their deceased. For instance, certain cultures have practiced cremation on funeral pyres, while others have opted for burial, and some have even left their dead to be consumed by wild animals in high places. These varied practices underscore the depth of cultural

3

significance and abstraction that different societies attach to the act of honoring the dead.

The practice of cremation on a funeral pyre, for example, often evokes images of the medieval Scandinavians, notably the Vikings. Their funerals were elaborate, theatrical, and steeped in ritual, reflecting a belief system that included various "halls of the dead," such as Folkvang and the famed Valhalla, reserved for warriors. These rites were designed to aid the deceased in their journey to the afterlife, with the level of ceremony reflecting the individual's social standing. Following the cremation, Vikings were often interred in burial mounds with their possessions, symbolizing their life achievements. This was typically followed by days of feasting and celebration, highlighting the communal aspect of mourning and remembrance.

Ground burial, another prevalent practice, dates back over 100,000 years, with evidence found in Neanderthal sites. Though we know little of the cultures that began this ritual, it is speculated that ground burial began as a strictly practical practice. After all, mucking about your toils of daily life and having to navigate decaying corpses in the process would have been very unpleasant, even to societies that used only stone, wood, and bone tools. At some point along the way, significance was assigned to certain aspects of this ritual, adopted and characterized primarily by religion regarding their beliefs in an afterlife. These range from

4

immediate covering and interment to public display and elaborate rites, often accompanied by religious readings or prayers to guide the deceased in the afterlife. The dynastic Egyptians, for example, are renowned for their meticulous body preparations and funeral rites, aimed at ensuring comfort in the afterlife.

Sky Burial, or *Jhator*, practiced in regions with heavy Buddhist populations such as Tibet and Mongolia, offers a distinct perspective on death. In this ritual, the deceased's body is left exposed to be consumed by scavengers, typically vultures, and the elements, symbolizing the body's return to the circle of life. This ritual is thought to have been birthed from practicality since most of Tibet's topography and geology make internment nearly impossible and being above the treeline makes cremation impractical. Buddhists believe strongly in the concept of being generous and compassionate to all creatures. It is this last act of returning the unused vessel through the circle of life that demonstrates that generosity.

These practices underscore the role of abstraction in human culture, demonstrating how societies attach symbolic meanings to rituals that, from a purely sensory or practical viewpoint, might appear interchangeable. This capacity for abstraction sets humans apart from the majority of the animal kingdom, suggesting that culture is a uniquely human phenomenon. While some behaviors observed in non-human

5

species hint at cultural elements, the depth of meaning and symbolism found in human cultural practices is unparalleled. As scientific understanding evolves, so too does our appreciation for the complexity of culture and the ways in which it enriches the human experience.

Throughout the early twentieth century, Anthropology experienced significant growth as a discipline, gaining widespread acceptance in academic institutions and expanding its conceptual framework through the integration of sociology, psychology, and other disciplines. This interdisciplinary approach led to a broadening understanding of culture, transitioning it from a static to a dynamic concept. Culture came to be recognized as a dynamic social construct, continuously shaped and reshaped by the behaviors of its members, which in turn, are influenced by the cultural norms established by the group.

The understanding of culture underwent a significant transformation during the twentieth century, with anthropologists revealing that culture is not a fixed entity but a living, breathing construct that constantly evolves. This evolution is driven by a cyclical process where culture prescribes behaviors to its members, and these behaviors, in turn, contribute to the enrichment and transformation of culture. This dynamic interplay ensures that culture remains in a state of flux, always leaning towards progression. The recognition of culture as an ever-changing phenomenon underscores the necessity of acknowledging its inherent malleability and the potential for cultural norms to shift over time. What may have been considered acceptable behavior within a society or group a decade ago may no longer hold the same status today, and vice versa.

The dynamic nature, malleability, and elasticity of culture are reflected in the evolution of societal customs as communities grow in size and sophistication. Embracing this malleability is crucial, as it allows culture to evolve gradually, facilitating change while preserving the unique customs that distinguish a society from its peers or competition. Without this capacity for slow, progressive change, cultures risk stagnation, which can lead to detrimental outcomes for society.

Cultural stagnation poses significant risks, including the stifling of progressive, innovative ideas and the eventual societal upheaval as younger generations seek to emulate the progress observed in neighboring societies. This desire for

7

change can lead to a hierarchical upheaval, characterized by rapid and often tumultuous transitions, potentially resulting in a complete overhaul of cultural norms. Societies experiencing such upheaval may find themselves unable to reconcile the conservative longing for the past with the progressive push for change, leading to internal conflict and vulnerability to external threats.

Several factors can influence the direction and pace of cultural change, including societal turmoil, technological advancements, and breakthroughs in science and knowledge. Historical events such as the United States civil rights movement and the space race illustrate how societal challenges and technological innovations can catalyze profound cultural shifts. These events not only required behavioral changes but also led to the establishment of new norms that define the culture we live in today, such as the reliance on GPS navigation, global communication free of language barriers, and access to information through AI-driven technologies.

The concept of culture, with its inherent dynamism and capacity for change, plays a pivotal role in shaping societies. Understanding culture as a fluid and evolving construct allows for the recognition of its adaptability in the face of societal changes, technological advancements, and shifts in collective knowledge. By fostering a culture that embraces progression and remains open to gradual change, societies can avoid the pitfalls of stagnation, ensuring their long-term success and sustainability. The history and evolution of cultural understanding teach us the importance of nurturing a living culture that is responsive to the needs and challenges of its time, thereby paving the way for a future where innovation, inclusion, and progress are celebrated.

The Culture Of Business

The parallels between societal culture and business culture are both profound and instructive. Just as the broader concept of culture influences and shapes societies, business culture plays a critical role in determining the trajectory and success of an organization. Understanding business culture as a dynamic and evolving entity can significantly enhance an organization's adaptability, resilience, and capacity for innovation in an ever-changing corporate landscape.

In the realm of business, culture encompasses the collective values, beliefs, and practices that define an organization and influence its operations. This culture is not static; it evolves in response to internal developments and external pressures, including technological advancements, market trends, and shifts in workforce demographics. Recognizing the fluidity of business culture is essential for organizations aiming to stay relevant and competitive. It enables companies to respond proactively to changes, rather than being overtaken by them.

The capacity for adaptability, fostered by a culture that values flexibility and innovation, is a hallmark of successful organizations. In the face of societal changes such as evolving consumer preferences or the advent of disruptive technologies, businesses with adaptable cultures are better positioned to pivot their strategies, adopt new technologies, and meet emerging market demands. This adaptability extends to internal processes and workforce management, allowing organizations to leverage the diverse skills and perspectives of their employees to drive growth and innovation.

A business culture that embraces progression and is open to gradual change can significantly mitigate the risks of stagnation. Stagnation in business can manifest as outdated business models, inefficient processes, or a disengaged workforce, all of which can hinder an organization's growth and profitability. By fostering a culture that not only accepts but actively seeks out opportunities for improvement and development, businesses can ensure their long-term viability and success.

The concept of nurturing a living, responsive business culture underscores the importance of continuous engagement with employees, stakeholders, and the market. This involves soliciting feedback, encouraging open dialogue, and being receptive to new ideas and perspectives. A living culture is one that evolves in alignment with the organization's strategic objectives while remaining grounded in core values that provide coherence and identity.

Leadership plays a pivotal role in shaping and sustaining a positive business culture. Leaders who demonstrate commitment to the organization's values, engage in transparent communication, and show genuine concern for employee well-being can inspire trust, loyalty, and

11

a sense of shared purpose. Effective leaders act as catalysts for cultural evolution, steering the organization through periods of change with a clear vision and a unifying sense of direction.

A future-oriented business culture celebrates innovation, inclusion, and progress. Innovation is encouraged as a means to develop new products, services, and ways of working that can provide a competitive edge. Inclusion is embraced to ensure that diverse voices and perspectives are valued, enhancing decision-making and problem-solving. Progress is pursued not just in terms of financial growth but also in contributing positively to society and the environment.

The parallels between societal and business cultures highlight the significance of adaptability, progression, and responsive leadership in ensuring organizational success. By understanding and nurturing a dynamic business culture, organizations can navigate the complexities of the modern business environment, fostering innovation, inclusion, and sustainable growth. Just as societies thrive when they embrace change and progress, so too do businesses when they cultivate a culture that is vibrant, adaptable, and aligned with the evolving needs of their employees, customers, and the broader community.

History of Business Culture

The concept of corporate culture has evolved significantly over time, paralleling changes in the broader social, economic, and technological landscapes. Its history can be segmented into several key phases.

In the early 20th century, the landscape of business culture was significantly shaped by the burgeoning Industrial Revolution, which heralded a shift towards mass production and the mechanization of labor. This period was characterized by a fervent emphasis on industrial efficiency, with companies zealously adopting the principles of scientific management—a theory developed by Frederick W. Taylor, often considered the father of industrial engineering. Taylor's principles were revolutionary, focusing on optimizing worker productivity through meticulous time and motion studies. This approach sought to break down tasks into their most basic elements and then systematically analyze and streamline these components to increase efficiency and output.

13

The advent of scientific management marked a profound transformation in the way work was organized and performed. Taylor's approach was grounded in the belief that there existed a single 'best way' to perform any given task. By identifying this optimal method and training workers to follow it precisely, productivity could be maximized. This method involved detailed observation and measurement of tasks, with the aim of eliminating unnecessary movements and standardizing work processes across the board.

The implications of scientific management extended beyond the mere mechanics of task execution. It introduced a level of discipline and control over the workforce that was previously unattainable, fundamentally altering the relationship between management and labor. Managers began to assume a more authoritative role, armed with scientifically derived data to dictate work methods and pace.

While scientific management brought significant advancements in operational efficiency, it was not without its drawbacks. The intense focus on productivity and the mechanization of labor led to a de-emphasis of the human aspect of work. Workers were often viewed as mere cogs in the industrial machine, valued primarily for their physical output rather than their overall well-being or job satisfaction. This reductionist view of labor led to a range of issues, including worker dissatisfaction, fatigue, and a lack of engagement.

Critics of scientific management argued that the approach failed to account for the complexity and variability of human behavior. Workers, they contended, were not automatons that could be programmed for maximum efficiency but individuals with diverse needs, motivations, and capacities. The disregard for these human elements sparked debates and discussions that would eventually contribute to the evolution of business culture.

The limitations of scientific management and the growing awareness of its impact on workers led to a gradual shift in business culture. By the mid-20th century, theories and practices began to emerge that placed greater emphasis on the human aspects of work. This shift marked the beginning of a more holistic approach to managing work and workers, acknowledging that productivity and efficiency could not be sustained without considering the well-being and engagement of the workforce.

The early 20th century was a pivotal period in the development of business culture, marked by a drive for industrial efficiency through the principles of scientific management. While this approach yielded significant improvements in productivity, it also highlighted the importance of balancing operational efficiency with the human aspects of work. The lessons learned from this era have informed subsequent developments in business culture, underscoring the need for approaches that harmonize the goals of the organization with the needs and aspirations of its employees.

The Human Relations Movement

The Human Relations Movement, spanning from the 1930s to the 1950s, represented a seminal shift in the understanding and management of work within the corporate world. This period was characterized by a growing recognition of the complex interplay between the psychological and social dimensions of work and their profound impact on organizational productivity and employee satisfaction. The movement emerged as a response to the mechanistic and efficiency-focused approaches of the early 20th century, most notably scientific management, which largely ignored the human element of labor.

The movement's genesis is often traced back to the groundbreaking research conducted by Elton Mayo and his colleagues at the Hawthorne Works of the Western Electric Company in the late 1920s and early 1930s. The Hawthorne studies initially aimed to examine the effects of physical working conditions on employee productivity but inadvertently uncovered the significant role of social factors and worker perceptions. One of the most notable findings was the "Hawthorne Effect," which suggested that workers were more motivated and productive when they sensed their work was being observed and deemed important by management. This revelation underscored the importance of social relations, employee morale, and the psychological contract between employers and employee.

The insights gleaned from the Hawthorne studies and the broader Human Relations Movement catalyzed a profound transformation in management practices. Organizations began to pay greater attention to the needs and well-being of their employees, recognizing that job satisfaction and a sense of belonging could significantly enhance productivity. Leadership styles evolved, with a greater emphasis on empathy, communication, and the cultivation of positive workplace relationships. Managers were encouraged to adopt a more participative approach, involving employees in decision-making processes and fostering a sense of ownership and involvement in organizational goals.

A central tenet of the Human Relations Movement was the link between employee morale and productivity. The movement posited that satisfied, psychologically fulfilled employees were more engaged and efficient, contributing to a positive organizational climate and enhanced performance. This perspective advocated for a more holistic approach to work, one that balanced task requirements with social and emotional needs. Practices such as team-building activities, recognition programs, and opportunities for personal development became integral components of organizational culture, aimed at bolstering morale and fostering a supportive, inclusive work environment.

The Human Relations Movement laid the groundwork for modern organizational behavior and human resource

18

management practices. Its emphasis on the psychological and social aspects of work continues to influence contemporary business culture, informing approaches to leadership, team dynamics, and employee engagement. The movement's legacy is evident in the ongoing focus on creating positive work environments that respect and nurture the human elements of labor, recognizing that the well-being of employees is inextricably linked to the success of the organization.

These years marked a pivotal era in the evolution of business culture, shifting the paradigm from a narrow focus on efficiency and mechanization to a more comprehensive understanding of the workplace as a social system. By highlighting the importance of psychological and social factors, the movement fundamentally altered the way organizations approach the management of work and workers, laying the foundation for a more humane, empathetic, and effective business culture.

Corporate Culture Boom

The 1980s marked a transformative period in the realm of business culture, known as the Corporate Culture Boom. This era was characterized by a burgeoning interest in the intangible elements that underpin organizational effectiveness and success. The concept of corporate culture, which encompasses the shared values, beliefs, and practices that shape the behavior and identity of an organization, became a focal point of discussion among business leaders, scholars, and consultants. This shift in focus was significantly influenced by seminal publications that challenged prevailing notions about the determinants of organizational performance.

Two landmark books published during this time, "Corporate Cultures: The Rites and Rituals of Corporate Life" by Terrence Deal and Allan Kennedy, and "In Search of Excellence" by Tom Peters and Robert H. Waterman Jr., played pivotal roles in elevating the importance of corporate culture within the business community. These works argued compellingly that the success of an organization extends beyond its strategies, structures, or systems to include the strength and alignment of its culture. They posited that a strong, cohesive culture could enhance employee motivation, foster commitment, and drive higher levels of performance.

"Corporate Cultures" introduced the idea that rituals, ceremonies, and the informal side of the organization significantly influence employee behavior and attitudes. Deal and Kennedy highlighted the importance of understanding and harnessing these cultural elements to achieve strategic goals and enhance organizational effectiveness.

"In Search of Excellence," on the other hand, presented case studies of companies that had achieved outstanding performance by focusing on people, customers, and values. Peters and Waterman's work underscored the critical role of leadership in shaping a positive, value-driven culture that could propel an organization to excellence.

The Corporate Culture Boom underscored the role of leadership in cultivating and maintaining a strong corporate culture. Leaders were recognized as the principal architects of culture, responsible for articulating a clear vision and values that could guide the behavior and decision-making of employees. Effective leaders were those who could not only define the desired culture but also embody and reinforce it through their actions, communication, and decision-making processes.

During the 1980s, corporate culture began to be seen as a source of competitive advantage. Organizations with strong, positive cultures were believed to be better positioned to attract and retain talent, adapt to change, and achieve superior performance. The era brought a heightened awareness of the need to align culture with business strategy, ensuring that the values, norms, and practices of the organization supported its strategic objectives and market positioning.

The shift in awareness during the 1980s has left a lasting legacy on the field of business management. The insights from this era have informed subsequent theories and practices related to organizational development, change management, and leadership. The emphasis on corporate culture as a critical component of organizational success continues to influence contemporary business practices, with companies increasingly investing in initiatives to understand, shape, and leverage their cultures.

The 1980s represented a pivotal moment in the evolution of business culture, with the Corporate Culture Boom bringing the concept of corporate culture to the forefront of organizational strategy. The era's seminal works and the subsequent focus on the role of leadership in shaping culture have fundamentally altered the way businesses approach the creation and management of their cultural environments. As organizations continue to navigate an ever-changing business landscape, the lessons from the Corporate Culture Boom remain relevant, underscoring the importance of cultivating a strong, aligned corporate culture to achieve lasting success and sustainability.

Globalization

The era from the 1990s to the present has been marked by significant shifts in the global business landscape, characterized by an increased emphasis on globalization, diversity, and inclusion. This period has witnessed businesses across the globe acknowledging and leveraging the multifaceted benefits of cultivating diverse and inclusive corporate cultures. Coupled with the advent and proliferation of the internet and digital communication technologies, these cultural shifts have profoundly transformed how organizations operate, collaborate, and compete on the global stage.

Globalization has expanded the markets and operational territories for businesses, necessitating a more nuanced understanding and appreciation of cultural differences. Organizations have increasingly sought to establish a presence in multiple countries, navigating a complex web of cultural, legal, and economic environments. This global expansion has underscored the importance of cultural adaptability and sensitivity, driving companies to integrate global perspectives into their strategic planning and day-to-day operations. As a result, corporate cultures have evolved to become more inclusive of diverse customs, traditions, and business practices, enhancing their ability to operate seamlessly across borders.

The late 20th and early 21st centuries have also underscored the intrinsic value of diversity and inclusion within the workplace. Businesses have come to recognize that a diverse workforce — one that includes a wide range of ethnicities, genders, ages, religions, sexual orientations, and cultural backgrounds — brings a wealth of perspectives, ideas, and experiences that can drive innovation and creativity. Inclusion efforts have focused on ensuring that all employees feel valued and empowered to contribute their best work, irrespective of their background or identity. By fostering an environment where diversity is celebrated and inclusion is prioritized, organizations have tapped into deeper wells of creativity, problem-solving, and innovation, gaining a competitive edge in an increasingly complex and interconnected world.

The digital revolution, marked by the rise of the internet and digital communication tools, has further catalyzed changes in corporate culture. The widespread adoption of digital technologies has enabled more flexible work arrangements, including remote work, telecommuting, and virtual teams. This shift has not only expanded the talent pool available to organizations but has also prompted a reevaluation of traditional work models and a greater focus on work-life balance. Digital platforms have facilitated real-time communication and collaboration across geographical boundaries, breaking down silos within and between organizations. The transformation towards digital-centric work cultures has demanded adaptability, continuous learning, and an openness to change from employees and leaders alike.

As part of the cultural shift towards greater flexibility and inclusivity, there has been a pronounced emphasis on work-life balance. Organizations have increasingly acknowledged the importance of supporting employees' well-being, both within and outside the workplace. Initiatives aimed at promoting work-life balance — such as flexible working hours, wellness programs, and support for family commitments — have become integral to corporate cultures, reflecting a holistic approach to employee satisfaction and retention.

The era from the 1990s to the present has been a period of profound change and evolution in business culture, driven by the forces of globalization, diversity, inclusion, and digitalization. Organizations that have embraced these changes have not only enhanced their operational effectiveness and innovation capacity but have also positioned themselves as attractive employers for a diverse and talented workforce. As the business landscape continues to evolve, the lessons learned during this era about the value of inclusivity, adaptability, and the integration of technology will remain crucial for organizations seeking to thrive in an increasingly complex and dynamic global market.

The Digital Age

The Digital Age represents a pivotal era in the evolution of business culture, characterized by rapid technological advancements and significant shifts in workplace dynamics. This period, within which we currently reside, has seen an accelerated move towards digitalization, profoundly impacting how organizations operate, communicate, and innovate. The COVID-19 pandemic only hastened these changes, compelling businesses to adapt to new realities and reevaluate their cultural priorities.

In the Digital Age, agility has become a critical attribute for organizations aiming to navigate the fast-paced technological landscape successfully. Businesses have recognized the need to be flexible and responsive to changes in market conditions, consumer behaviors, and technological innovations. This emphasis on agility has led to a cultural shift where decision-making processes are streamlined, and hierarchies are flattened, enabling quicker responses to emerging opportunities and challenges.

Innovation, too, has taken center stage, with companies striving to foster a culture that encourages creativity, experimentation, and risk-taking. The digital era has opened up new avenues for innovation, from product development and customer engagement strategies to operational efficiencies and business models. Organizations that cultivate a culture supportive of innovation are better positioned to leverage technological advancements and maintain a competitive edge.

The Digital Age has also brought sustainability to the forefront of business culture. As societal awareness of environmental issues has increased, so has the expectation for businesses to operate responsibly and sustainably. Companies are increasingly embedding sustainability into their corporate cultures, recognizing that long-term success depends on their ability to minimize environmental impact, promote social responsibility, and govern ethically. This shift towards sustainability not only reflects a moral commitment but also aligns with the growing consumer preference for brands that demonstrate genuine concern for the planet and its inhabitants.

The COVID-19 pandemic dramatically accelerated the adoption of remote work, fundamentally altering corporate cultures worldwide. Organizations have had to quickly adapt

27

to a dispersed workforce, leading to a greater reliance on digital tools and platforms for communication and collaboration. This transition has underscored the importance of digital literacy and has prompted businesses to invest in technologies that facilitate effective remote work.

Digital collaboration has become a cornerstone of the modern workplace, enabling teams to work together seamlessly regardless of geographical location. This has expanded the talent pool available to organizations, allowing them to attract and retain skilled employees from across the globe. The move towards digital collaboration has also fostered a culture of inclusivity, where diverse perspectives can be more easily integrated into decision-making processes and project development.

Perhaps one of the most significant cultural shifts in the Digital Age has been the renewed focus on employee well-being and mental health. The challenges associated with remote work, such as isolation, burnout, and the blurring of work-life boundaries, have highlighted the need for organizations to support their employees' physical and psychological health. Businesses are increasingly implementing programs and policies aimed at promoting

28

work-life balance, offering mental health resources, and creating a supportive work environment. This focus on well-being is not only essential for the health of employees but also contributes to higher levels of engagement, productivity, and retention.

The Digital Age has ushered in a new era of business culture, marked by agility, innovation, sustainability, digital collaboration, and an emphasis on employee well-being. As organizations navigate the complexities of the digital landscape, the ability to adapt and evolve culturally will be paramount. The businesses that thrive in this era will be those that recognize the importance of fostering a culture that is responsive to technological advancements, committed to sustainability, and supportive of the holistic well-being of their employees.

Throughout its history, business culture has reflected broader societal values and economic conditions, adapting to the changing needs of workers and the marketplace. Today, a strong, positive corporate culture is considered a critical component of organizational success, attracting talent, driving engagement, and fostering a competitive edge in a rapidly changing world.

Chapter 2: The Foundation of Leadership

The cornerstone of any thriving corporate culture is its leadership. Leadership does more than merely steer the operational direction of an organization; it molds, shapes, and defines the very ethos of a company's environment. Leaders who demonstrate integrity, transparency, and empathy inspire their employees to emulate these qualities. Furthermore, leaders who actively listen to their team members and show genuine interest in their well-being establish a culture of trust and respect. Effective leadership also involves setting clear expectations and providing the necessary resources for employees to achieve their goals. Each of these elements plays a crucial role in creating a supportive, inclusive, and high-performing work environment that fosters a sense of belonging and security. Leadership transcends the mere guidance of an organization's operational trajectory; it fundamentally sculpts, influences, and defines the essence of the company's culture.

At the heart of impactful leadership lies the trio of integrity, transparency, and empathy. Leaders endowed with integrity act as ethical compasses, guiding their organizations with honesty and moral principle. Such leaders not only adhere to ethical standards themselves but also instill these values within their teams, fostering an environment where ethical conduct is the norm. Transparency from leadership, in turn, cultivates a culture of openness. By communicating openly about the organization's operations, decisions, and challenges, leaders demystify the decision-making process, making it accessible and understandable to all employees. This transparency builds trust within the team, as members feel informed and included in the organization's journey.

Empathy, the third pillar, involves understanding and genuinely caring for the well-being of employees. Empathetic leaders recognize the challenges and pressures their team members may face and strive to create a supportive work environment. Such leaders celebrate the individuality of their team members, acknowledging and accommodating their diverse needs and aspirations. This empathy strengthens the bond between leaders and their teams, fostering a sense of mutual respect and understanding.

Leaders who engage in active listening demonstrate to their teams that their ideas, feedback, and concerns are

31

valued. Active listening involves more than just hearing words; it requires understanding, processing, and responding thoughtfully to the input received. By actively listening, leaders can identify and address issues proactively, engage in meaningful problem-solving, and make their team members feel seen and heard. Furthermore, showing genuine interest in the well-being and professional development of employees reinforces the idea that the organization cares about its members not just as workers but as individuals. This approach helps to establish a culture of trust and respect, where employees feel secure and valued.

Effective leadership also encompasses the setting of clear expectations and the provision of necessary resources to meet these expectations. Leaders must articulate the organization's goals and their vision for how these goals can be achieved, ensuring that each team member understands their role in this process. Clear expectations eliminate ambiguity and align team efforts towards common objectives. Moreover, equipping employees with the necessary resources—be it training, tools, or support—enables them to perform their roles effectively and confidently. This empowerment not only enhances productivity but also contributes to employee satisfaction and engagement, as team members feel supported in their endeavors.

The culmination of these leadership qualities and practices is the creation of a supportive, inclusive, and high-performing work environment. Such an environment fosters a sense of belonging and security among employees, encouraging them to bring their best selves to work. An inclusive culture values diversity and provides equal opportunities for all employees to grow, contribute, and excel. This inclusivity, supported by effective leadership, drives performance and innovation, as diverse perspectives and skills come together to propel the organization forward.

Leadership is the linchpin of a thriving corporate culture. Leaders who embody and practice integrity, transparency, empathy, active listening, and who set clear expectations while providing necessary resources, lay the groundwork for a supportive, inclusive, and high-performing work environment. These leadership qualities foster a culture of trust, respect, and belonging, which is essential for the long-term success and sustainability of any organization. Through committed and effective leadership, organizations can cultivate environments that not only drive performance and innovation but also ensure the well-being and satisfaction of their employees.

The Role of Integrity

Integrity stands as a non-negotiable pillar of effective leadership. Leaders who exhibit integrity in their decisions, communications, and interactions set a powerful example for the entire organization. This integrity fosters an environment where honesty is valued, ethical behavior is the norm, and doing the right thing is prioritized over easy or expedient choices. When leaders uphold these standards, they cultivate a culture where employees feel secure in upholding these same values, knowing that their actions are in alignment with the organization's core principles.

Integrity in leadership transcends mere ethical compliance; it embodies the essence of moral leadership and accountability. When leaders consistently demonstrate integrity, they not only set a high ethical standard but also create a ripple effect throughout the organization, encouraging a culture of trust and reliability. This is because integrity acts as the cornerstone of trust; employees are more

34

likely to trust and follow leaders who are transparent, honest, and consistent in their actions and decisions. Such trust is crucial for fostering an open and collaborative work environment where team members feel confident in their leaders' guidance and in the direction in which the organization is headed.

Moreover, integrity shapes the organization's reputation both internally and externally. In an era where consumers and employees alike value corporate social responsibility and ethical conduct, a leadership team that prioritizes integrity helps bolster the organization's image and attracts like-minded individuals and partners. This alignment between words and actions reassures stakeholders of the organization's commitment to ethical practices, enhancing its credibility and appeal in the competitive marketplace.

Leaders who navigate challenges with integrity also inspire resilience and ethical problem-solving among their teams. By valuing doing the right thing over short-term gains, they model how to face ethical dilemmas and make tough decisions without compromising on core values. This leadership approach ensures that the organization not only thrives in the present but is also well-equipped to sustain its success and ethical standing in the long run, making integrity not just a moral choice, but a strategic imperative for enduring success.

Integrity in leadership embodies the commitment to consistently align actions with a set of moral principles, even when faced with challenging circumstances. Leaders with integrity navigate the complex landscape of organizational life by making decisions that are not only legally compliant but also ethically sound. This unwavering commitment to doing what is right over what is convenient or beneficial in the short term sets a moral compass for the entire organization to follow. Such leaders become beacons of ethical guidance, demonstrating through their actions that integrity is not situational but a steadfast commitment to uphold one's values irrespective of the circumstances.

The influence of leaders who prioritize integrity extends beyond their immediate decisions; it permeates the entire organizational culture. When leadership exemplifies integrity, it sends a clear message about the organization's values, establishing a standard for what is expected from every team member. This consistency between espoused values and actions reinforces the importance of ethical behavior, creating an environment where honesty and accountability are not just encouraged but are ingrained in the organizational DNA. Employees, mirroring the integrity displayed by their leaders, are more likely to conduct themselves with honesty and uphold the organization's ethical standards, fostering a culture where ethical dilemmas are approached with a principled mindset.

At the heart of a collaborative and high-performing team lies trust—trust that is significantly influenced by the integrity of its leaders. When leaders demonstrate transparency, honesty, and consistency, it builds a foundation of trust that is critical for effective teamwork and communication. Employees who trust their leaders are more open to sharing ideas, taking risks, and engaging in constructive conflict, knowing that their contributions are valued and their welfare is a priority. This trust extends beyond internal dynamics, impacting how the organization collaborates with partners, stakeholders, and the broader community. By prioritizing integrity, leaders cultivate a climate of trust that enhances collaboration, drives innovation, and ensures that the organization can navigate challenges with unity and resilience.

In today's interconnected and socially conscious marketplace, an organization's reputation is one of its most valuable assets. Leadership integrity plays a pivotal role in shaping how the organization is perceived externally. Consumers and potential partners are increasingly evaluating organizations not just on their products or services but on their ethical stance and the behavior of their leadership. Organizations led by individuals who embody integrity are more likely to be viewed positively, attracting customers, investors, and employees who share similar values. This alignment between an organization's ethical practices and societal expectations bolsters its reputation, making it a preferred choice for those looking to engage with businesses that prioritize ethical conduct and social responsibility.

The true test of integrity comes when organizations face adversity. Leaders who stand firm in their ethical principles during crises demonstrate a level of resilience that serves as a model for the entire organization. By choosing the harder right over the easier wrong, leaders not only solve problems ethically but also inspire their teams to approach challenges with a similar level of moral fortitude. This approach to problem-solving ensures that the organization not only survives difficult times but emerges stronger, with its ethical integrity intact. Moreover, navigating challenges with integrity prepares the organization for future obstacles, embedding a sense of moral resilience that becomes a key component of its identity and strategy.

Viewing integrity not just as a moral choice but as a strategic imperative is crucial for long-term success. In an era characterized by rapid change and increasing ethical scrutiny, organizations that are anchored in strong ethical principles are better positioned to adapt and thrive. Integrity leads to decisions that are sustainable and aligned with long-term goals, ensuring that the organization builds a legacy of ethical excellence. As such, integrity in leadership is not merely about maintaining a moral high ground; it is about embedding ethical considerations into the strategic fabric of the organization, ensuring its actions are not only profitable but also principled.

The role of integrity in leadership is multifaceted and profound, extending from the foundation of ethical decision-making to shaping organizational culture, fostering trust and collaboration, enhancing external reputation, and inspiring resilience. Leaders who embody integrity set a powerful example, creating a ripple effect that strengthens the moral fiber of the entire organization. As the business landscape continues to evolve, the importance of integrity remains constant, serving as both a moral guide and a strategic asset. Organizations led by individuals committed to upholding integrity are not only equipped to navigate the complexities of the modern world but are also poised to lead the way in building a more ethical, responsible, and sustainable future.

The Essence of Transparency in Leadership

The concept of transparency in leadership has become a cornerstone of modern organizational culture, reflecting a shift towards more open, honest, and accountable management practices. This paradigm shift recognizes the value of making organizational processes, decisions, and challenges visible to all members of a company, fostering an environment of trust, engagement, and shared responsibility. Expanding on this concept involves exploring the multifaceted role of transparency in enhancing trust, promoting employee engagement, encouraging accountability, and ultimately contributing to the organization's success.

Transparency in leadership is fundamentally about fostering open communication and visibility regarding the company's operations, strategic decisions, and the challenges it faces. This openness is critical in demystifying the decision-making process, allowing employees to see the rationale behind executive decisions and how these decisions align with the company's broader objectives and values. By involving employees in this way, leaders not only empower their workforce but also instill a sense of belonging and purpose, key ingredients for a motivated and cohesive team.

Trust is the foundation of any strong relationship, including the relationship between leaders and their teams. Transparency is a powerful tool for building this trust, as it signals to employees that leaders value honesty and are committed to the welfare of both the individuals and the organization as a whole. When leaders share information openly, especially in times of uncertainty or change, they demonstrate vulnerability and confidence in their team's ability to handle the truth, which, in turn, strengthens the team's trust in leadership. This trust is crucial for creating a secure work environment where employees feel safe to express their ideas, concerns, and feedback.

Employee engagement and commitment are significantly influenced by their understanding of and alignment with the company's direction and decisions. Transparency in leadership ensures that employees are not just executing tasks but are actively participating in the company's journey, aware of how their individual roles contribute to larger goals. This understanding fosters a sense of ownership and pride in their work, motivating employees to put forth their best effort. Furthermore, when employees are informed about the challenges the company faces and are invited to contribute their ideas and solutions, they are more likely to feel valued and engaged, driving higher levels of commitment and performance.

Accountability is another critical aspect of a healthy organizational culture that is reinforced by transparency. When leaders are open about expectations, responsibilities, and the impact of each team member's work, it creates a culture where accountability is not just expected but embraced. Transparent leadership practices, such as sharing performance metrics, setting clear goals, and providing constructive feedback, help ensure that everyone understands their role in the organization's success. This clarity not only helps in aligning individual efforts with the company's objectives but also encourages employees to take ownership of their actions and their outcomes.

Transparency in leadership also plays a pivotal role in encouraging innovation and effective problem-solving within the organization. When leaders are open about challenges and actively seek input from their teams, it creates a collaborative environment where diverse ideas and perspectives are valued. This openness stimulates creativity and innovation, as employees feel empowered to suggest new approaches and solutions without fear of criticism. Moreover, by fostering a culture where challenges are openly discussed, leaders can harness the collective intelligence of their team to navigate obstacles more effectively and drive the organization forward.

While the benefits of transparency in leadership are clear, navigating the challenges it presents requires careful consideration. Leaders must balance the need for openness with the responsibility to protect sensitive information and maintain strategic confidentiality. Additionally, being transparent, especially about difficult decisions or organizational changes, requires strong communication skills and emotional intelligence. Leaders must be able to convey information in a way that is both honest and compassionate, ensuring that employees feel supported rather than anxious or demoralized.

Implementing transparency in leadership involves more than just an intention to be open; it requires specific practices and behaviors that promote visibility and communication. This can include regular updates on company performance, open forums for discussion and feedback, transparent decision-making processes, and clear communication during times of change. Additionally, leaders should actively encourage and model transparency, demonstrating through their actions the value of openness and setting the tone for the rest of the organization to follow.

Transparency in leadership is a critical element of a healthy, thriving organizational culture. It builds trust, enhances employee engagement, fosters accountability, encourages innovation, and strengthens the overall success of the organization. By embracing transparency, leaders can create an environment where employees are informed, involved, and invested in the company's journey. However, achieving true transparency requires deliberate actions and a commitment to open, honest communication, underpinned by the courage to share not just successes but also challenges and failures. As organizations continue to navigate an increasingly complex and dynamic business environment, the importance of transparency in leadership has never been more evident, serving as a key differentiator in attracting and retaining talent, building resilience, and driving sustainable growth.

Understanding Empathy in Leadership

Empathy, often overlooked in traditional models of leadership, has emerged as a critical virtue in the contemporary workplace. This shift reflects a deeper understanding of the complex human dynamics that underpin organizational success. Empathy in leadership transcends mere professional courtesy; it is an intentional effort to understand and appreciate the experiences, challenges, and motivations of employees. By fostering a culture of empathy, leaders can cultivate an environment where employees feel genuinely supported, leading to enhanced satisfaction, loyalty, and performance.

Empathy in leadership is characterized by a leader's ability to step into the shoes of their employees, understand their feelings and perspectives, and use that understanding to guide their actions. This empathetic engagement requires more than just listening; it involves active engagement, asking thoughtful questions, and demonstrating genuine concern for team members' well-being. When leaders practice empathy, they signal to their employees that they are seen, heard, and valued not just as contributors to the organization's goals but as individuals with unique experiences and needs.

Employee satisfaction is significantly influenced by the quality of interactions with leadership. Empathetic leaders, by acknowledging the individuality of their team members, create a work environment where employees feel respected and valued. This respect and valuation are not limited to professional achievements but extend to personal well-being and challenges. Such an environment fosters a positive emotional connection to the workplace, enhancing overall job satisfaction. When employees feel that their leaders care about them as individuals, they are more likely to feel content with their jobs, leading to lower turnover rates and a more stable, committed workforce. Loyalty, a critical component of organizational success, is deeply rooted in the emotional

46

bonds between employees and their leaders. Empathy strengthens these bonds by demonstrating to employees that their leaders are invested in their success and well-being. This investment goes beyond mere transactional relationships, where loyalty is contingent on rewards or recognition, to foster a sense of belonging and commitment to the leader's vision and the organization's goals. Loyalty cultivated through empathy is resilient, enduring through challenges and changes because it is based on mutual respect and understanding.

Empathy contributes to enhanced performance by addressing the holistic needs of employees. Leaders who understand the pressures and challenges faced by their team members can provide targeted support, resources, and flexibility, enabling employees to perform at their best. Furthermore, empathetic leadership encourages a culture of open communication, where employees feel comfortable sharing ideas and concerns. This openness leads to innovative problem-solving, effective collaboration, and a collective commitment to quality and excellence. By valuing and responding to the human element of the workforce, empathetic leaders unlock the full potential of their teams.

Developing empathy as a leadership virtue requires intentional practice and reflection. Leaders can enhance their empathetic abilities by engaging in active listening, being present in conversations, and showing genuine interest in the lives of their team members. This practice involves not only understanding the challenges employees face but also celebrating their successes and acknowledging their efforts. Additionally, leaders can foster empathy by encouraging a culture of feedback, where employees feel safe to express their thoughts and feelings without fear of judgment or reprisal.

Empathy plays a crucial role in navigating the complexities of a diverse workplace. By embracing empathy, leaders can appreciate the varied backgrounds, experiences, and perspectives of their team members. This appreciation is essential for creating an inclusive environment where all employees feel valued and understood. Empathetic leadership is particularly important in addressing issues of equity and inclusion, as it allows leaders to recognize and address biases, barriers, and disparities within the organization. By championing empathy, leaders can ensure that diversity is not just tolerated but celebrated as a source of strength and innovation.

While the benefits of empathy in leadership are clear, implementing this approach can present challenges. One of the primary obstacles is the misconception that empathy equates to leniency or a lack of discipline. However, empathy in leadership is not about lowering standards or excusing poor performance; it is about understanding the factors that contribute to challenges and working collaboratively to find solutions. Additionally, leaders may struggle with balancing empathy with the need to make tough decisions. Navigating this balance requires transparency, clear communication, and a commitment to fairness, ensuring that decisions are made with consideration for the impacts on all stakeholders.

As the workplace continues to evolve, the demand for empathetic leadership will only grow. The challenges of the modern work environment, including remote work, digital communication, and global teams, underscore the need for leaders who can navigate the emotional and relational complexities of their organizations. Empathetic leadership, with its focus on understanding, caring, and connection, offers a blueprint for building resilient, adaptive, and human-centered organizations. In the future, the most successful leaders will be those who recognize the power of empathy in unlocking the potential of their teams and fostering an environment where everyone can thrive.

Empathy as a leadership virtue is indispensable in the contemporary workplace. It is the key to building relationships of trust, enhancing employee satisfaction and loyalty, and driving performance. By practicing empathy, leaders can create a supportive work environment that acknowledges the whole person, leading to a more engaged, committed, and productive workforce. As organizations face increasing complexity and change, empathetic leadership will be critical in navigating these challenges with humanity and grace. The future of leadership is empathetic, and those who embrace this virtue will lead the way in building organizations that are not only successful but also genuinely enrich the lives of those they serve.

Active Listening in Leadership

Active listening, often heralded as a cornerstone of effective communication, emerges as a pivotal skill in the arsenal of successful leadership. This nuanced form of listening transcends mere auditory reception, embodying a comprehensive engagement with the speaker's message, both verbally and non-verbally. For leaders, mastering the art of active listening signals a profound respect for their team's perspectives, fostering an environment where dialogue, innovation, and collaboration flourish.

Active listening in leadership encapsulates a deliberate focus and genuine engagement with the speaker's message. It involves attentively hearing the speaker, processing the information, and providing thoughtful feedback or responses. This process requires the listener to be fully present, setting aside distractions and preconceptions to truly understand the speaker's intent and emotions. For leaders, active listening is not just a communication tool but a leadership strategy that values and validates the voices of team members, fostering a sense of belonging and respect within the organization.

One of the most significant impacts of active listening is the empowerment of employees. When leaders actively listen, they convey to their team members that their thoughts, concerns, and ideas are important and worthy of attention. This validation encourages employees to speak up, share their insights, and contribute more actively to the organization's goals. Empowered employees are more engaged, motivated, and satisfied with their jobs, leading to higher levels of performance and commitment to the organization. Furthermore, by fostering an open dialogue, leaders can tap into the diverse perspectives and skills of their team, unlocking potential and driving innovation.

Active listening is instrumental in cultivating a culture of innovation and continuous improvement within organizations. By genuinely listening to and considering the ideas and feedback of employees, leaders can foster an environment that encourages creative thinking and problem-solving. This openness to new ideas and willingness to engage in constructive dialogue about improvements and changes signals to employees that innovation is valued and supported. Such a culture not only generates innovative solutions to challenges but also continuously seeks ways to enhance processes, products, and services, keeping the organization competitive and adaptive in a rapidly changing market.

Leaders who excel in active listening are better equipped to identify and address issues before they escalate into significant problems. By understanding the nuances of a concern or conflict through active listening, leaders can engage in more effective problem-solving and conflict resolution. This skill allows leaders to gather a comprehensive understanding of the situation, including underlying causes and potential impacts, enabling them to devise solutions that are thoughtful, equitable, and sustainable. Moreover, active listening during conflict resolution helps to maintain respect and trust among team members, ensuring that conflicts are resolved in a manner that strengthens team dynamics rather than undermining them.

Active listening plays a vital role in building a cohesive and motivated team. When team members feel heard and understood by their leaders, it strengthens their trust in leadership and their commitment to the team's objectives. This sense of belonging and mutual respect enhances team dynamics, making it easier for members to collaborate, support one another, and work towards common goals. Furthermore, active listening facilitates clearer communication, reducing misunderstandings and ensuring that everyone is aligned with the team's direction and priorities. A cohesive and motivated team is more resilient, adaptable, and capable of achieving high levels of performance.

Implementing active listening in leadership requires intentional practice and reflection. Leaders can develop their active listening skills through several strategies, including focusing fully on the speaker, avoiding interruptions, reflecting on the speaker's message, asking clarifying questions, and providing feedback that shows understanding and appreciation of the speaker's perspective. Additionally, leaders can create opportunities for active listening through regular one-on-one meetings, team discussions, and feedback sessions, ensuring that all team members have a voice and feel valued.

Despite its importance, active listening can be challenging to practice consistently. Common obstacles include distractions, preconceived notions, and emotional reactions that can hinder full engagement with the speaker's message. Leaders must be aware of these challenges and actively work to overcome them, such as by minimizing distractions during conversations, practicing mindfulness to stay present, and developing emotional intelligence to manage personal reactions. By addressing these challenges, leaders can enhance their active listening skills and foster more meaningful and productive interactions with their teams.

Active listening is a critical leadership virtue that has far-reaching implications for organizational success. By practicing active listening, leaders demonstrate respect and value for their team members' contributions, empowering employees, fostering a culture of innovation, facilitating effective problem-solving, and enhancing team cohesion and motivation. Despite the challenges it may present, the benefits of active listening in leadership underscore its significance as a tool for building stronger, more responsive, and more cohesive teams. In an era where effective communication is more important than ever, the ability to listen actively stands as a hallmark of effective, empathetic, and transformative leadership.

Chapter 3: Clear Expectations in Organizational Success

Setting clear expectations stands as a pivotal component of effective leadership and a critical determinant of an organization's success. This leadership practice is instrumental in fostering an environment of heightened productivity, focused efforts, and strategic congruence across various levels of the organization. By clearly articulating expectations, leaders provide a framework within which team members can operate with confidence and clarity, aligning their individual contributions with the collective objectives of the organization.

The establishment of clear expectations is more than a managerial task; it is a leadership imperative that underpins the operational and strategic fabric of an organization. It serves as a foundation for building a culture of accountability, transparency, and mutual respect. When leaders articulate precisely what is expected in terms of performance, behavior, and outcomes, it does more than guide employees; it empowers them. This empowerment comes from understanding how one's role contributes to the broader organizational goals, fostering a sense of purpose and belonging among team members.

At the heart of setting clear expectations is the act of effective communication. Leaders must ensure that their message is not only conveyed but also understood and internalized by their team members. This involves a clear articulation of the goals, the standards by which performance will be evaluated, and the behaviors that are valued by the organization. Such communication acts as a navigational compass, guiding employees through their daily tasks and aligning their personal ambitions with the organization's overarching objectives. It is through this alignment that individuals can navigate their path toward personal and professional growth while contributing to the collective success of the organization.

The process of setting clear expectations plays a crucial role in eliminating ambiguity and potential confusion within the workplace. Ambiguity in roles, responsibilities, or goals can lead to inefficiencies, frustration, and a dilution of efforts. By establishing clear expectations, leaders ensure that all team members are synchronized in their efforts, working towards a common goal with a shared understanding of what success looks like. This clarity fosters a sense of cohesion and unity, making it easier for teams to collaborate, innovate, and navigate challenges collectively.

Strategic alignment is another critical outcome of setting clear expectations. When individual roles and responsibilities are aligned with the organization's strategic objectives, it ensures that every action taken by employees contributes to the broader vision of the organization. This alignment is essential for maintaining organizational agility, allowing the organization to respond effectively to changes in the external environment, capitalize on opportunities, and mitigate risks. Furthermore, strategic alignment enhances organizational prosperity by optimizing resource allocation, focusing efforts on high-impact activities, and driving sustained performance.

Setting clear expectations is not merely a leadership strategy but a cornerstone of organizational prosperity. It facilitates heightened productivity, strategic alignment, and a cohesive understanding among team members of their roles and responsibilities. Effective communication of these expectations acts as a critical navigational tool, guiding employees towards the achievement of both personal ambitions and organizational goals. By eliminating ambiguity and fostering a unified vision of success, leaders can enhance the overall cohesion, agility, and performance of their organization. As such, the practice of setting clear expectations is indispensable for leaders seeking to cultivate an environment of excellence and drive their organization towards long-term success.

Enhancing individual and collective performance is a critical goal for any organization aiming for success and sustainability in today's competitive landscape. Clear expectations play a vital role in achieving this objective, serving as a catalyst for optimizing productivity, efficiency, and team synergy. They equip employees with a roadmap, guiding their daily activities and strategic efforts toward achieving defined objectives. This clarity cuts through the noise of competing priorities, enabling individuals to focus their energies on tasks that directly contribute to organizational goals. A focused approach to work not only enhances productivity but also increases job satisfaction, as employees can see the tangible results of their efforts and understand their role in the broader organizational narrative.

Understanding what is expected allows employees to prioritize their tasks more effectively. In an environment where priorities are constantly shifting, clear expectations act as a stabilizing force, helping individuals to distinguish between urgent and important tasks. This discernment is crucial for efficient time management and resource allocation, ensuring that critical objectives are met within set

59

timelines, and resources are utilized in the most impactful manner.

When employees are clear about what is expected of them, they are more likely to pursue their objectives with a heightened sense of purpose. This sense of purpose is deeply motivating, driving individuals to excel in their roles and contribute to the organization's success. Furthermore, understanding how one's work fits into the larger organizational goals fosters a sense of belonging and significance, further fueling motivation and engagement.

The alignment of individual efforts with organizational goals through clear expectations leads to increased synergy within teams. This synergistic effect amplifies the impact of collaborative efforts, as team members work cohesively towards common objectives. The collaborative environment fostered by clear expectations encourages the sharing of ideas, knowledge, and best practices, leading to innovative solutions and improved performance.

Setting clear expectations plays a crucial role in minimizing potential conflicts and duplication of efforts within teams. When each team member understands their specific role and how it contributes to the team's objectives, the likelihood of overlapping responsibilities and the resultant friction is significantly reduced. This clarity promotes a harmonious working environment where energy is focused on productive endeavors rather than resolving internal disputes or redundancies.

The collective understanding and pursuit of shared goals, facilitated by clear expectations, enhance team performance and cohesion. This unity is critical for achieving complex objectives that require the integration of diverse skills and perspectives. Moreover, a cohesive team is more resilient in the face of challenges, capable of adapting and overcoming obstacles through collective effort and mutual support.

To maximize the positive impact on individual and collective performance, leaders must employ effective strategies in setting and communicating expectations. This involves engaging in open and continuous dialogue with team members to ensure that expectations are understood and agreed upon. Additionally, incorporating SMART (Specific, Measurable, Achievable, Relevant, Time-bound) criteria in goal-setting can provide a clear and objective framework for evaluating performance.

A culture of accountability, supported by clear expectations, ensures that individuals and teams take ownership of their performance and outcomes. This accountability, coupled with recognition of achievements, reinforces the value of meeting and exceeding expectations, motivating continued excellence and improvement.

Setting clear expectations is not a one-time event but an ongoing process that requires regular review and adjustment. Providing continuous feedback allows for real-time adjustments to expectations in response to changing circumstances or objectives, ensuring that individuals and teams remain aligned with organizational goals.

The establishment of clear expectations is a powerful lever for enhancing individual and collective performance within an organization. By providing a focused approach to work, enabling effective prioritization, and fostering a heightened sense of purpose, clear expectations drive productivity and efficiency at the individual level. Simultaneously, on a collective level, clear expectations increase team synergy, minimize conflict and duplication, and enhance overall team performance and cohesion. Implementing strategies for setting clear expectations, fostering a culture of accountability and recognition, and providing continuous feedback are essential steps in leveraging this dynamic to achieve organizational success. Through these efforts, organizations can create an environment where clarity, alignment, and purpose propel both individuals and teams towards exemplary performance and significant achievements.

Fostering a Culture of Accountability

Fostering a culture of accountability within an organization is a transformative strategy that amplifies performance, nurtures trust, and aligns individual actions with collective goals. This culture is predicated on the clear articulation of expectations, providing employees with a definitive framework for evaluating their contributions and outcomes.

At the heart of an accountability culture lies the clear definition of expectations. When leaders articulate what is expected in terms of performance, behavior, and results, they lay down a benchmark that serves as a reference point for all organizational activities. This clarity is crucial, as it demystifies what success looks like and outlines the pathways to achieving it. Moreover, it empowers employees by providing them with the autonomy to take ownership of their roles and responsibilities, fostering a sense of agency and purpose.

Accountability transcends the basic notion of task completion to encompass the ownership of outcomes. This broader perspective encourages employees to not only fulfill their duties but also to consider the broader impact of their actions on the organization's success. In an environment where accountability is prized, employees feel motivated to exceed expectations, innovate, and make decisions that further the organization's objectives. This empowerment is a catalyst for growth, prompting individuals to embrace challenges, seek continuous improvement, and contribute to a culture of excellence.

Leaders play a pivotal role in fostering a culture of accountability. Through their actions, leaders model accountability, demonstrating a commitment to organizational values and objectives. They also set the tone by holding themselves accountable, which in turn sets expectations for the behavior and performance of their teams. Furthermore, leaders facilitate accountability by providing the necessary resources, support, and feedback that employees need to succeed. This leadership approach is instrumental in creating an environment where accountability is viewed as a shared value and a collective commitment.

Building a culture of accountability requires deliberate and sustained effort. Key strategies include:

- Setting Clear Expectations: Clearly articulated expectations form the foundation of accountability. Leaders must ensure that these expectations are specific, measurable, achievable, relevant, and time-bound (SMART) to provide a clear direction for employee performance.
- Encouraging Ownership: Employees should be encouraged to take ownership of their roles and the outcomes of their work. This involves granting them autonomy to make decisions, solve problems, and contribute ideas that drive organizational success.
- Providing Regular Feedback: Continuous feedback is essential for reinforcing accountability. Constructive

feedback helps employees understand how their actions align with organizational goals and where improvements can be made.

- Recognizing and Rewarding Accountability: Acknowledging and rewarding employees who demonstrate accountability reinforces its value within the organization. Recognition programs can motivate others to exhibit similar behaviors.
- Creating a Supportive Environment: A culture of accountability flourishes in an environment that supports risk-taking and learning from failure. Leaders should foster an atmosphere where employees feel safe to experiment, innovate, and learn from their experiences.

A culture of accountability is closely linked to trust within the organization. When employees and leaders consistently meet and exceed expectations, it builds confidence in each other's commitment to the organization's success. This trust is reciprocal; employees trust leaders to provide direction and support, while leaders trust employees to fulfill their responsibilities and contribute to organizational objectives. Such trust enhances communication, collaboration, and cohesion across the organization, further solidifying the culture of accountability.

Accountability has a profound impact on organizational performance. It ensures that all employees are aligned with the organization's goals and are actively contributing to its success. This alignment results in increased efficiency, higher productivity, and improved outcomes. Moreover, accountability fosters innovation, as employees feel empowered to explore new ideas and approaches that can drive the organization forward. Ultimately, a culture of accountability positions the organization for sustainable growth and competitiveness.

Despite its benefits, establishing a culture of accountability can present challenges. Resistance may arise from a fear of failure or a misunderstanding of what accountability entails. To overcome these obstacles, leaders must clearly communicate the benefits of accountability, provide training and resources to support employee development, and create a safe environment where mistakes are viewed as opportunities for learning and growth.

Fostering a culture of accountability is a strategic imperative for organizations aiming to enhance performance, build trust, and achieve their goals. By setting clear expectations, empowering employees, providing regular feedback, and recognizing accountability, leaders can cultivate an environment where accountability is valued and practiced by all. Such a culture not only drives organizational success but also contributes to a positive and engaging workplace where employees are committed to excellence and innovation. Through deliberate effort and sustained commitment, leaders can transform accountability into a defining characteristic of their organizational culture, paving the way for lasting success and growth.

Facilitating Feedback and Growth

Facilitating feedback and growth within an organization is a dynamic process that significantly contributes to the development of a robust, adaptable, and competitive workforce. The establishment of clear expectations forms the bedrock of this process, serving as a crucial framework for the delivery and reception of constructive feedback. This framework ensures that feedback is not only meaningful and actionable but also aligned with the strategic objectives of the organization.

The articulation of clear expectations is fundamental to the feedback process. It delineates the parameters of success, enabling employees to align their efforts with the organization's goals. When expectations are explicitly stated, employees possess a clearer understanding of their roles and the standards against which their performance will be evaluated. This clarity transforms feedback from a potentially ambiguous or subjective critique into a valuable tool for professional development. Employees are better positioned to contextualize feedback within the scope of their roles and responsibilities, facilitating a more receptive and proactive approach to their personal and professional growth.

Constructive feedback is a cornerstone of effective employee development. It bridges the gap between current performance and potential excellence, offering insights into areas of strength and opportunities for improvement. Constructive feedback, when delivered within the framework of clear expectations, becomes a powerful motivator for employees. It encourages them to reflect on their

69

performance, recognize their accomplishments, and identify areas where they can enhance their skills and competencies. This reflective process is critical for personal and professional growth, as it prompts employees to undertake continuous learning and actively seek opportunities for development.

An organizational culture that values clear expectations and regular feedback naturally cultivates an environment where risk-taking and innovation are encouraged. When employees understand the benchmarks for success and the parameters within which they can operate, they feel more secure in exploring new ideas and approaches. This security stems from the knowledge that their experimentation is supported by a framework designed to guide their growth and development. Such an environment not only nurtures individual creativity and innovation but also enhances the organization's overall adaptability and competitiveness. Employees who are encouraged to push boundaries and explore uncharted territories contribute to a dynamic organizational culture that is capable of responding to changing market demands and emerging opportunities.

Implementing effective feedback and growth strategies requires a thoughtful and systematic approach. Leaders can facilitate this process by:

- Establishing a Continuous Feedback Loop: Feedback should be an ongoing dialogue rather than a sporadic or annual event. Regular check-ins and performance discussions ensure that feedback is timely, relevant, and aligned with evolving expectations.
- Focusing on Specific, Actionable Insights: Feedback is most effective when it is specific and actionable. Leaders should provide concrete examples and practical advice that employees can implement to improve their performance and achieve their development goals.
- Promoting a Growth Mindset: Encouraging employees to adopt a growth mindset helps them view feedback as an opportunity for learning rather than a critique of their abilities. This perspective fosters resilience, openness to feedback, and a commitment to continuous improvement.
- Leveraging Diverse Feedback Sources: Incorporating feedback from multiple sources, including peers,

direct reports, and cross-functional partners, provides employees with a comprehensive view of their performance and impact. This 360-degree feedback approach enriches the development process and highlights the interconnectedness of roles within the organization.

The facilitation of feedback and growth has a profound impact on organizational success. It drives performance improvement, enhances employee engagement, and fosters a culture of excellence and accountability. Employees who receive regular, constructive feedback and are supported in their growth efforts are more likely to be engaged, motivated, and committed to the organization's objectives. Additionally, an organizational culture that prioritizes personal and professional development attracts and retains top talent, further strengthening the organization's competitive edge.

Despite its benefits, facilitating effective feedback and growth can present challenges, including resistance to feedback, variations in individual learning styles, and the need for ongoing support and resources. Overcoming these challenges requires leaders to cultivate an environment of trust and openness, tailor development opportunities to individual needs, and provide consistent support and resources that enable employees to pursue their growth objectives.

The facilitation of feedback and growth within the context of clear expectations is a dynamic and transformative process that significantly enhances individual and organizational performance. By establishing a framework for success, providing meaningful and actionable feedback, and promoting an environment conducive to risk-taking and innovation, organizations can foster a culture of continuous improvement and adaptability. This culture not only supports the personal and professional development of employees but also positions the organization for sustained success and competitiveness in an ever-evolving business landscape. Through deliberate and strategic efforts to facilitate feedback and growth, organizations can unlock the full potential of their workforce, driving performance, engagement, and innovation to new heights.

Implementing Clear Expectations

Ultimately, the practice of setting clear expectations is a powerful driver in the attainment of organizational goals. By ensuring that all team members are aligned with the organization's vision and understand their contribution to its success, leaders can mobilize their workforce towards common objectives. This alignment ensures that efforts are not wasted on unproductive or misaligned activities, optimizing the organization's resources and energy.

Clear expectations also facilitate strategic planning and execution. When leaders set specific, measurable, achievable, relevant, and time-bound (SMART) expectations, they lay out a roadmap for success that can be followed at all levels of the organization. This strategic approach not only ensures that short-term objectives are met but also that the organization is positioned for long-term success.

Implementing clear expectations within an organization is a nuanced process that necessitates strategic communication, consistent reinforcement, and an unwavering commitment to transparency. This methodology is crucial for cultivating an environment where every team member is not only aware of what is expected of them but is also fully equipped to meet these expectations.

The cornerstone of implementing clear expectations is the ability of leaders to communicate these expectations in a manner that is both understandable and accessible. This clarity in communication serves to eliminate any ambiguity, ensuring that all team members have a precise understanding of what is expected in terms of their roles, responsibilities, and the standards against which their performance will be measured. To achieve this level of clarity, leaders must employ a communication strategy that is inclusive and considers the diverse backgrounds and learning styles of their team members. This may involve the use of multiple communication channels, such as meetings, emails, and visual aids, to convey expectations in a manner that resonates with everyone. Furthermore, providing a rationale for these expectations helps employees understand their importance and relevance to the organization's objectives, fostering a deeper sense of commitment and purpose.

The dynamic nature of business necessitates that expectations, once set, are not static but subject to regular review and adjustment. This flexibility ensures that expectations remain relevant and aligned with the evolving goals of the organization. Regular check-ins and updates serve as critical touchpoints for reinforcing expectations and addressing any discrepancies between expected and actual performance. These interactions also provide an avenue for feedback, allowing employees to voice concerns, seek clarification, and suggest adjustments based on their experiences and insights. Such a collaborative approach to managing expectations not only reinforces their importance but also demonstrates a leader's commitment to supporting their team's success.

Transparency is a critical element in the implementation of clear expectations. It involves open and honest communication about the organization's goals, the rationale behind specific expectations, and how individual contributions fit into the larger picture. A transparent approach builds trust, as team members feel valued and respected when leaders share information openly. Moreover, transparency in discussing progress and challenges related to meeting expectations fosters a culture of accountability, where successes are celebrated, and setbacks are viewed as opportunities for learning and growth. This culture of openness encourages employees to take initiative, communicate more freely, and engage more deeply with their work and the organization.

Perhaps the most powerful tool in the implementation of clear expectations is leadership by example. Leaders must embody the behaviors, performance standards, and work ethic they expect from their team members. By demonstrating a commitment to the organization's values and objectives, leaders can inspire their teams to strive for excellence. This modeling of expectations sets a tangible benchmark for performance and conduct within the team, making the abstract concept of "expectations" concrete and achievable. Furthermore, when leaders hold themselves to the same standards they set for their teams, it reinforces the fairness and universality of these expectations, further solidifying the culture of accountability and excellence within the organization

To effectively implement clear expectations, leaders can employ several strategies, including:

- Developing a Clear Communication Plan: This plan should outline how expectations will be communicated, the channels that will be used, and how understanding and buy-in will be assessed.

- Establishing Mechanisms for Regular Feedback: Creating structured opportunities for feedback ensures that there is ongoing dialogue about expectations, performance, and areas for improvement.
- Fostering a Supportive Environment: Encouraging a team culture that supports risk-taking, innovation, and continuous learning can make meeting expectations a collective endeavor rather than an individual challenge.

The implementation of clear expectations is a multi-faceted process that requires deliberate action and sustained effort from organizational leaders. Through articulate communication, regular reinforcement, a commitment to transparency, and leading by example, leaders can create an environment where expectations are not only clear but also embraced and internalized by team members. This alignment between individual roles and organizational objectives is essential for driving performance, fostering a culture of accountability, and ultimately achieving the organization's goals. By prioritizing the implementation of clear expectations, leaders can unlock the full potential of their teams and guide their organizations toward sustained success and growth.

Overcoming Challenges

Overcoming challenges in setting and maintaining clear expectations is a pivotal aspect of effective leadership and organizational management. While the benefits of clear expectations are well-documented, ranging from enhanced productivity to improved alignment with organizational goals, the journey toward establishing such clarity is often fraught with obstacles. These challenges can stem from a variety of sources, including resistance to change, fear of failure, lack of resources, and communication barriers.

Resistance from employees can manifest in various forms, often as a reaction to the perceived threat of change or the fear of increased accountability. This resistance is not inherently negative but can be an expression of underlying concerns or uncertainties. Leaders must approach resistance with empathy, seeking to understand the root causes.

79

Whether it stems from a deeply ingrained organizational culture that valorizes autonomy over structured guidance, or from individual insecurities about meeting heightened standards, recognizing the source of resistance is the first step in addressing it.

Creating an environment where open communication thrives is essential for overcoming resistance to clear expectations. Leaders should initiate dialogues that allow employees to express their concerns and reservations freely. This openness not only helps in identifying specific points of resistance but also in demonstrating leadership's willingness to listen and adapt. Regular forums, such as team meetings, one-on-one sessions, and feedback platforms, can facilitate this exchange, ensuring that communication flows both ways. Within this communicative space, the rationale behind setting specific expectations can be clarified, demystifying the process and aligning it more closely with individual and team values.

Another significant challenge in implementing clear expectations is ensuring that employees have the necessary support and resources to meet these standards. Leaders must recognize that setting expectations without providing the means to achieve them can lead to frustration and demotivation. Addressing this challenge requires a proactive approach to resource allocation, including training programs that equip employees with the skills needed to succeed, mentorship opportunities that offer guidance and support, and access to the tools and information essential for task completion. By investing in employee development, leaders signal their commitment to the workforce's growth, fostering a culture where meeting expectations is viewed as a shared goal rather than an individual burden.

The fear of failure is a potent barrier to meeting clear expectations. To mitigate this fear, leaders should cultivate a culture that values learning and adaptability over perfection. This cultural shift involves recognizing and celebrating efforts, even when they fall short of the desired outcome, and viewing mistakes as opportunities for growth. Encouraging risk-taking within reasonable boundaries and providing constructive feedback on failures can help employees internalize the idea that growth is a continuous process, and setbacks are part of the journey toward excellence.

Overcoming challenges in setting and maintaining clear expectations also involves continuously reinforcing their value to both the individual and the organization. Leaders can achieve this through regular success stories that highlight how clear expectations have led to personal and team achievements, thereby making the abstract concept more tangible and relatable. Additionally, integrating the discussion of expectations into the fabric of organizational life—through performance reviews, reward systems, and professional development plans—can help solidify their importance and ensure they remain a focal point of organizational culture.

Leadership by example is perhaps the most powerful tool in overcoming challenges related to clear expectations. When leaders themselves embody the behaviors, attitudes, and performance standards they expect from their teams, they provide a living blueprint for success. This demonstration of commitment not only inspires confidence but also builds trust, making it easier for employees to align their actions with organizational expectations.

Addressing the challenge of equipping employees to meet expectations necessitates a commitment to continuous learning and development. Tailored training programs that address specific skills gaps, leadership development initiatives that prepare employees for future roles, and continuous learning opportunities that keep the workforce abreast of industry trends are all critical components of this strategy. By prioritizing education and development, organizations can ensure their employees are not only prepared to meet current expectations but are also equipped to adapt to future challenges.

Setting clear expectations emerges as a cornerstone of effective leadership and a pivotal factor in the equation of organizational triumph. This leadership tenet, underscored by the precise articulation of desired performance metrics, behavioral standards, and anticipated outcomes, serves as a catalyst for a multitude of organizational benefits. From elevating productivity levels to nurturing a culture steeped in accountability, the practice of setting clear expectations plays a critical role in shaping the operational and strategic landscape of an organization. Moreover, it lays the groundwork for constructive feedback mechanisms and personal development pathways, ultimately steering the organization toward the realization of its overarching ambitions.

The implementation of clear expectations is not a one-time event but a dynamic process that demands strategic communication, continuous reinforcement, and unwavering dedication to leading by example. Leaders are tasked with not only defining and communicating these expectations but also embodying them, thereby setting a benchmark for their teams. This leadership approach facilitates a transparent and cohesive work environment where every team member is aligned with the organization's goals and empowered to contribute meaningfully.

While the journey of instilling clear expectations may encounter obstacles, from resistance to change to communication gaps, the enduring benefits far eclipse these transient challenges. Among the most significant advantages is the enhancement of individual and team performance. Clear expectations eliminate ambiguity, enabling employees to channel their efforts more effectively and align their contributions with the organization's strategic direction. This alignment is instrumental in fostering a sense of purpose and motivation among employees, driving them to excel in their roles.

Additionally, a culture of accountability emerges within an organization where clear expectations are the norm. This culture encourages individuals to take ownership of their responsibilities and outcomes, fostering a proactive and results-oriented workforce. The clarity provided by well-defined expectations also paves the way for meaningful feedback and growth opportunities. Employees and leaders alike can engage in constructive dialogues centered on performance and development, promoting continuous improvement and adaptability.

Ultimately, the practice of setting clear expectations is integral to driving the achievement of organizational goals. By providing a clear direction and establishing a framework for evaluation, organizations can ensure that their collective efforts are geared toward success. The strategic alignment facilitated by clear expectations not only enhances operational efficiency but also fosters innovation and resilience, enabling the organization to navigate the complexities of the modern business landscape.

The establishment of clear expectations stands as a linchpin in the realm of effective leadership and organizational success. It engenders a multitude of benefits, from heightened productivity and accountability to the facilitation of feedback and personal growth, culminating in the successful attainment of organizational objectives. Despite potential challenges, the strategic implementation of clear expectations, underscored by effective communication and leadership by example, remains an indispensable practice for leaders aiming to cultivate excellence and drive their organizations toward sustained success.

Chapter 4: Providing Necessary Resources

The allocation and management of resources within an organization are critical responsibilities that fall under the purview of effective leadership. This essential function goes beyond the mere distribution of tools and equipment; it is about strategically equipping the workforce with a comprehensive array of resources including advanced technologies, vital information, targeted training programs, mentorship opportunities, and robust support systems. Such a holistic approach to resource provision is instrumental in fostering an environment conducive to employee growth, driving innovation, and ensuring the successful realization of organizational goals.

At the heart of resource provision is the objective of nurturing employee growth and development. By offering access to educational and training opportunities, leaders can facilitate continuous learning and skill enhancement, enabling employees to advance in their careers and contribute more effectively to the organization. Mentorship programs, in particular, play a crucial role in this developmental process, offering guidance, advice, and support that can help individuals navigate the complexities of their roles and the broader industry landscape. This focus on personal and professional development not only benefits the employees but also enriches the organization by cultivating a highly skilled and knowledgeable workforce.

Innovation is a key driver of competitive advantage and long-term success in today's rapidly evolving business environment. The provision of state-of-the-art tools and technologies is essential for fostering an innovative culture within an organization. Leaders must ensure that their teams have access to the latest digital platforms, software, and other technological resources that can facilitate creative problem-solving, streamline operations, and enhance product and service offerings. Additionally, by encouraging an open exchange of ideas and supporting experimental projects, organizations can harness the collective creativity of their employees, leading to breakthrough innovations that can redefine markets.

The overarching aim of providing necessary resources is to align employee capabilities and organizational objectives, ensuring that the workforce is equipped to meet the challenges and opportunities that lie ahead. This alignment is crucial for executing strategic plans and achieving desired outcomes. Effective leaders recognize that each resource—be it a tool, a piece of information, or a support system—serves as a building block in the foundation of organizational success. By carefully assessing the needs of their teams and deploying resources strategically, leaders can optimize performance across all levels of the organization, driving productivity, efficiency, and, ultimately, profitability.

Effective leadership is central to the successful provision of resources. Leaders must possess a deep understanding of their organization's goals, the specific needs of their teams, and the available resources that can address those needs. This requires a proactive and strategic approach to resource management, including the identification of gaps in capabilities, the evaluation of new technologies and methodologies, and the implementation of support structures that can facilitate employee success. Furthermore, leaders must cultivate an environment of trust and empowerment, where employees feel supported in their endeavors and confident in their ability to access and utilize the resources provided to them.

The provision of necessary resources within an organization is a multifaceted responsibility that is integral to effective leadership. By equipping employees with the tools, knowledge, training, and support they need, leaders can nurture employee growth, drive innovation, and align efforts towards the achievement of organizational objectives. This strategic approach to resource provision not only enhances individual performance but also contributes to the development of a resilient, agile, and forward-looking organization capable of navigating the challenges of the modern business landscape and seizing opportunities for sustained success.

The Strategic Imperative of Resource Provision

The strategic imperative of resource provision within an organization extends far beyond the mere allocation of tools and technologies; it embodies a leadership philosophy deeply committed to fostering individual growth and driving organizational success. This critical leadership function plays a pivotal role in enhancing operational efficiency, nurturing a competent and motivated workforce, and ensuring alignment with the organization's strategic goals. In today's rapidly evolving business landscape, characterized by relentless change and fierce competition, the ability to adapt and innovate is indispensable for securing a competitive edge.

Operational efficiency is a fundamental objective for any organization aiming to thrive in the competitive business environment. At the heart of achieving this efficiency is the provision of necessary resources, which enables employees to perform their duties effectively and efficiently. Tools, technology, and information act as catalysts that streamline processes, reduce redundancies, and minimize waste, thereby enhancing productivity and operational excellence. Leaders who prioritize resource provision ensure that their teams are not hamstrung by outdated or inadequate tools but are empowered with the best available resources to execute their tasks with precision and speed.

The provision of resources goes beyond the mere facilitation of day-to-day tasks; it is a critical investment in the workforce's competence and motivation. Training and development programs, for instance, equip employees with the skills and knowledge necessary to excel in their roles and adapt to new challenges. This investment in employee development signals to the workforce that the organization values their growth and is committed to their success. Such commitment from leadership fosters a motivated workforce that is not only competent in their current roles but also prepared to take on future challenges. Moreover, the availability of mentorship and support provides employees with the guidance and encouragement needed to navigate their career paths within the organization, further enhancing their engagement and loyalty.

Strategic alignment is the synchronization of organizational resources and activities with the company's long-term goals and strategic direction. The provision of necessary resources is critical in achieving this alignment, as it ensures that all employees are equipped to contribute effectively to the organization's objectives. By clearly articulating the strategic goals and providing the resources needed to achieve them, leaders create a cohesive environment where individual efforts collectively drive the organization forward. This alignment is especially crucial in today's dynamic business environment, where organizations must rapidly adapt to changes and seize new opportunities to maintain their competitive advantage.

The modern business landscape is marked by its complexity, characterized by technological advancements, shifting market dynamics, and evolving customer expectations. In such an environment, adaptability and innovation are not merely advantageous but essential for survival and success. The strategic provision of resources fosters an organizational culture that embraces change and encourages innovation. Employees empowered with the latest tools and technologies, and supported by a culture of continuous learning, are more likely to develop innovative solutions to challenges and contribute to the organization's adaptability. This culture of innovation, underpinned by strategic resource provision, enables organizations to navigate the complexities of the modern business landscape, responding swiftly to changes and capitalizing on emerging opportunities.

Leadership plays a decisive role in the strategic provision of resources. Effective leaders recognize the critical importance of equipping their teams with the necessary tools, training, and support to achieve organizational goals. This recognition involves not only identifying current resource needs but also anticipating future requirements in the context of evolving business strategies and market conditions. Leaders must, therefore, maintain a forward-looking perspective, continually assessing the external environment and internal capabilities to ensure that resource provision remains aligned with strategic objectives. Additionally, by fostering open communication and soliciting feedback from employees, leaders can gain valuable insights into resource gaps and areas for improvement, further enhancing the organization's strategic positioning.

The strategic provision of necessary resources is a testament to leadership's commitment to fostering individual growth and achieving organizational success. By equipping employees with the tools, training, and support they need, leaders enhance operational efficiency, cultivate a competent and motivated workforce, and ensure alignment with the organization's strategic goals. In the complex and dynamic modern business landscape, the ability to adapt and innovate is crucial for maintaining a competitive advantage. Therefore, the strategic imperative of resource provision is not merely an operational necessity but a fundamental pillar of organizational strategy, driving adaptability, innovation, and strategic alignment. Through thoughtful and proactive resource provision, leaders can navigate the challenges of the modern business environment, positioning their organizations for sustained success and growth.

Removing Barriers to Performance

Removing barriers to performance within an organization is an essential leadership responsibility that directly impacts productivity, employee satisfaction, and the

93

overall success of the company. These barriers can range from tangible obstacles, such as outdated technology and inadequate tools, to intangible challenges, including limited access to critical information and insufficient training. Addressing these barriers requires a proactive and strategic approach from leadership, demonstrating a commitment to fostering an environment where employees are equipped to excel in their roles.

The first step in removing barriers to performance is accurately identifying them. This process involves a thorough assessment of the workplace to pinpoint obstacles that prevent employees from performing at their best. Common barriers include outdated or inefficient technology that hampers productivity, lack of access to essential information needed for informed decision-making, and inadequate training programs that fail to equip employees with necessary skills and knowledge. Additionally, organizational processes and policies that are overly complex or bureaucratic can also act as significant impediments to performance. Leaders must engage in regular dialogue with employees, encouraging feedback to gain insights into the challenges they face and the resources they require to overcome these obstacles.

Providing the necessary resources to overcome identified barriers is crucial for enhancing productivity. Upgrading outdated technology and ensuring employees have access to the latest tools and software can dramatically increase efficiency, enabling employees to complete tasks more quickly and accurately. Similarly, creating systems that ensure easy access to critical information can streamline decision-making processes, allowing employees to make informed choices without unnecessary delays. Investing in comprehensive training programs is also vital, as it ensures employees possess the skills and knowledge to perform their roles effectively and adapt to new challenges as they arise.

Beyond improving productivity, removing barriers to performance significantly enhances employee satisfaction. When employees see that the organization is actively investing in resources that facilitate their work, it signals a commitment to their professional growth and success. This investment can lead to increased job satisfaction, as employees feel valued and supported by their employer. Moreover, by eliminating frustrations associated with inadequate resources, leaders can create a more positive and engaging work environment, contributing to higher levels of employee morale and reducing turnover rates.

95

Effective leadership is central to the successful removal of performance barriers. Leaders must adopt a proactive stance, anticipating potential obstacles and implementing strategies to mitigate them before they impact productivity. This requires a deep understanding of the organization's operational needs and the specific challenges faced by employees. Strategic planning, including regular reviews of technology and processes, ensures that resources remain aligned with the organization's goals and employees' needs. Leaders should also prioritize continuous improvement, seeking out opportunities to streamline operations and enhance efficiency through the strategic allocation of resources.

Removing barriers to performance not only addresses immediate challenges but also fosters a culture of innovation and adaptability within the organization. When employees are not bogged down by inefficiencies and have access to the tools and information they need, they are more likely to engage in creative problem-solving and explore innovative solutions to challenges. This culture of innovation can lead to significant advancements in products, services, and processes, driving the organization forward and maintaining its competitive edge in the market.

Leaders should also focus on implementing support systems that facilitate the removal of performance barriers. This includes creating clear channels for communication, where employees can report issues and request resources without fear of reprisal. Additionally, mentorship programs can provide employees with guidance and support as they navigate challenges, enhancing their ability to overcome obstacles and succeed in their roles.

The removal of barriers to performance is a critical leadership task that has profound implications for organizational productivity, employee satisfaction, and overall success. By proactively identifying and addressing obstacles, providing necessary resources, and fostering a culture of innovation and adaptability, leaders can create an environment where employees are empowered to perform at their best. This proactive approach not only demonstrates the organization's commitment to its workforce but also contributes to a more efficient, effective, and competitive organization. Through strategic planning, continuous improvement, and the implementation of support systems, leaders can ensure that their teams have the tools and support needed to overcome challenges and contribute to the organization's goals.

97

Removing barriers to performance within an organization is an essential leadership responsibility that directly impacts productivity, employee satisfaction, and the overall success of the company. These barriers can range from tangible obstacles, such as outdated technology and inadequate tools, to intangible challenges, including limited access to critical information and insufficient training. Addressing these barriers requires a proactive and strategic approach from leadership, demonstrating a commitment to fostering an environment where employees are equipped to excel in their roles. This essay explores the significance of removing performance barriers, the various forms these barriers can take, and the strategies leaders can employ to eliminate them, ultimately enhancing the efficiency and effectiveness of the workforce.

Identifying Barriers to Performance

Identifying barriers to performance within an organization is a critical first step toward enhancing efficiency, productivity, and overall employee satisfaction. This complex process demands a systematic approach to uncover the multifaceted obstacles that employees encounter in their daily operations. Barriers to performance can manifest in various forms, from tangible issues like outdated technology to more nuanced challenges such as organizational culture or lack of clear communication. By conducting a comprehensive assessment of the workplace and fostering an environment of open dialogue, leaders can pinpoint these barriers and develop strategies to mitigate them. This essay delves into the methods for identifying performance barriers, the common obstacles faced by employees, and the importance of leadership and employee feedback in this process.

The identification of performance barriers begins with a systematic assessment of the workplace. This evaluation should encompass all aspects of the organization's operations, including technology infrastructure, workflow processes, access to information, and the availability of training and development programs. Tools such as employee surveys, performance metrics, and workflow analysis can provide valuable data on where bottlenecks and inefficiencies occur. Additionally, examining industry benchmarks and best practices can help leaders understand how their organization's resources and processes compare to those of their competitors, highlighting areas for improvement.

99

Several common barriers often hinder employee performance, each requiring specific strategies to address:

- Outdated or Inefficient Technology: In an era where technological advancements occur rapidly, using outdated or inefficient technology can significantly slow down productivity. Employees struggling with slow systems or incompatible software are unable to perform tasks efficiently, leading to frustration and wasted time.

- Lack of Access to Essential Information: Effective decision-making is contingent upon having access to relevant and timely information. When employees lack this access, whether due to poor data management systems or restrictive information-sharing policies, it impedes their ability to make informed decisions and contributes to delays and errors.

- Inadequate Training Programs: The continuous development of skills and knowledge is fundamental to employee performance. Inadequate training programs that fail to address the evolving needs of the workforce or the demands of the market place employees at a disadvantage, limiting their potential and hampering organizational growth.

- Complex or Bureaucratic Processes and Policies: Overly complex procedures or bureaucratic hurdles can stifle innovation and agility within an organization. Employees bogged down by red tape or convoluted processes are less likely to take initiative or propose innovative solutions, leading to a stagnant organizational culture.

Effective leadership is paramount in the process of identifying barriers to performance. Leaders must cultivate a culture of transparency and open communication, where employees feel valued and heard. Engaging in regular dialogue with employees, through forums such as town hall meetings, suggestion boxes, and one-on-one conversations, allows leaders to gather firsthand insights into the obstacles that employees face. This feedback is invaluable, as it provides a direct window into the day-to-day challenges that may not be apparent from a management perspective.

Leaders should also be proactive in seeking feedback, asking specific questions about the tools and resources employees need to perform their roles more effectively. This proactive approach demonstrates leadership's commitment to removing barriers and improving the workplace environment.

Once barriers to performance have been identified, the next step involves developing targeted strategies to address them. This may include investing in new technology, revising information-sharing policies, enhancing training programs, or streamlining processes to reduce bureaucracy. Each strategy should be tailored to the specific needs of the organization and its employees, with clear objectives and timelines for implementation.

Identifying and addressing barriers to performance is an ongoing process. As such, leaders must continuously monitor the effectiveness of implemented strategies and be willing to adjust them as necessary. This iterative process ensures that the organization remains responsive to the evolving needs of its workforce and the changing dynamics of the business environment.

Identifying barriers to performance is a foundational step in fostering a productive, efficient, and satisfied workforce. Through a systematic assessment of the workplace and open dialogue with employees, leaders can pinpoint the obstacles that hinder performance and develop strategies to mitigate them. By addressing common barriers such as outdated technology, lack of access to information, inadequate training, and bureaucratic processes, organizations can unlock the full potential of their employees. Ultimately, the commitment of leadership to this process and their willingness to act on feedback and continuously refine their strategies are crucial for achieving organizational success and maintaining a competitive edge in the modern business landscape.

.

Enhancing Productivity Through Resource Provision

Enhancing productivity through the strategic provision of resources is a fundamental aspect of organizational success. This process involves not only the elimination of barriers that impede efficiency but also the empowerment of employees to perform at their optimum capacity. By upgrading outdated technology, ensuring access to the latest tools and software, streamlining access to critical information, and investing in comprehensive training programs, organizations can significantly boost productivity.

103

In the digital age, the role of technology in driving productivity cannot be overstated. Outdated or inefficient technology not only slows down operations but also frustrates employees, leading to decreased motivation and job satisfaction. By upgrading to the latest technology and ensuring employees have access to the tools and software they need, organizations can drastically improve efficiency. Modern tools designed with user experience in mind can simplify complex tasks, automate repetitive processes, and facilitate collaboration both within and across teams. This not only enables employees to complete their tasks more quickly and accurately but also frees up their time to focus on more strategic, value-added activities.

Access to relevant, timely information is crucial for effective decision-making. In many organizations, however, information silos and cumbersome data retrieval processes can severely hamper employees' ability to access the information they need. By creating systems that ensure easy access to critical information, organizations can streamline decision-making processes. This might involve implementing integrated data management systems, adopting cloud storage solutions for ease of access, or developing internal knowledge bases that serve as centralized repositories of information.

Such systems not only minimize delays but also enhance the quality of decisions by ensuring they are based on the most accurate and up-to-date information available.

The rapid pace of technological advancement and the constantly evolving business landscape demand that employees continually update their skills and knowledge. Comprehensive training programs are essential for ensuring that employees not only possess the foundational skills required for their current roles but are also equipped to tackle new challenges as they arise. These programs should cover a broad spectrum of needs, from technical skills specific to the tools and technologies used in the organization to soft skills such as communication, leadership, and problem-solving. Investing in employee training not only enhances productivity by improving competence and efficiency but also contributes to employee engagement and retention by demonstrating the organization's commitment to their professional development.

Enhancing productivity through resource provision is not a one-time endeavor but a continuous process that requires a cultural commitment to ongoing improvement. Organizations should foster an environment where feedback is actively sought and valued, where employees feel empowered to suggest improvements to tools, processes, and training programs. This culture of continuous improvement encourages innovation, as employees are motivated to identify and implement solutions that can further enhance productivity and efficiency.

While the benefits of providing necessary resources are clear, organizations may face challenges in implementing these strategies, including budgetary constraints, resistance to change, and the need to balance short-term costs with long-term benefits. Overcoming these challenges requires a strategic approach that prioritizes investments based on their potential impact on productivity and organizational goals. It also necessitates effective change management practices to ensure that employees are engaged and supportive of new initiatives.

In today's fast-paced and ever-evolving business landscape, the strategic provision of necessary resources emerges as a cornerstone for organizations striving to enhance productivity, drive innovation, and maintain a competitive edge. This approach entails a multifaceted commitment to upgrading technology and tools, facilitating seamless access to critical information, and investing in comprehensive training programs that collectively empower employees to excel in their roles. Such measures are not merely operational enhancements; they are vital investments in the human capital that constitutes the lifeblood of any organization.

The continuous advancement of technology offers organizations unprecedented opportunities to improve operational efficiency and productivity. By regularly assessing and upgrading their technological infrastructure, companies can ensure that their employees are equipped with the most effective tools available. This could range from state-of-the-art software that automates routine tasks to cutting-edge platforms that facilitate collaboration and innovation. The right technology can significantly reduce the time and effort required to complete tasks, freeing employees to focus on higher-value activities that contribute more directly to the organization's strategic goals.

In the information age, the ability to quickly and easily access relevant data and insights can significantly impact decision-making and productivity. Organizations that invest in systems and processes to streamline information access empower their employees to make informed decisions swiftly. This includes implementing integrated data management systems, fostering a culture of transparency and knowledge sharing, and ensuring that all employees have the training needed to effectively utilize these resources. Streamlined access to information not only accelerates the decision-making process but also enhances the quality and outcomes of those decisions.

The importance of ongoing professional development cannot be overstated. Comprehensive training programs that cover technical skills, industry knowledge, and soft skills are crucial for preparing employees to meet current and future challenges. Such programs not only enhance the competency and versatility of the workforce but also signal to employees that the organization is invested in their growth and career advancement. This investment in employee development fosters a culture of continuous learning and improvement, driving innovation and adaptability within the organization.

The provision of necessary resources, coupled with a supportive and empowering work environment, significantly enhances job satisfaction and employee engagement. When employees feel equipped to perform their duties effectively and are provided with opportunities for growth and development, they are more likely to be engaged with their work and committed to the organization's success. This heightened engagement translates into higher productivity, reduced turnover, and a more positive workplace culture, contributing to the overall success and sustainability of the organization.

The pivotal role of resource provision in organizational success underscores the need for it to be a key focus of strategic planning. Leaders must take a proactive and thoughtful approach to identifying the resources their teams need to succeed, both in the immediate and long-term future. This requires a deep understanding of the organization's strategic objectives, the challenges and opportunities present in the external environment, and the potential of the workforce. By prioritizing resource provision, leaders can ensure that their organization remains agile, innovative, and well-positioned to capitalize on new opportunities.

Enhancing productivity through the strategic provision of necessary resources is an essential strategy for organizations aiming to thrive in the complex and competitive business environment of today and tomorrow. By committing to the continuous upgrading of technology and tools, streamlining access to critical information, and investing in comprehensive training programs, organizations can empower their employees to achieve peak performance. This approach not only boosts productivity but also fosters job satisfaction and engagement, driving the collective success of the organization. As such, leaders must recognize resource provision as a crucial element of their strategic planning, ensuring their teams are fully equipped to navigate the challenges and seize the opportunities that lie ahead.

Chapter 5: Clear Values and Open Communication

A thriving and dynamic business culture is the linchpin of organizational success, rooted deeply in a bedrock of clear, shared values that permeate every aspect of decision-making and behavior. These foundational values serve as a compass, guiding the company in a direction that resonates with its core mission and vision. For this culture to flourish, it is imperative that these values are not only established with precision but are also communicated with unwavering clarity and consistency from the leadership to all levels of the organization. When employees have a profound understanding of these values and see their work as a reflection of them, they are more likely to forge a strong connection with the organization's purpose, driving their motivation and commitment to contribute to its overarching success.

The establishment of clear values, coupled with the fostering of open communication, stands as the cornerstone of a healthy business culture. These critical elements serve as the lifeblood of the organizational ecosystem, influencing not just the day-to-day interactions and operational choices but also molding the organization's long-term path. This chapter aims to explore the multifaceted role of these foundational elements in cultivating a robust corporate culture. It will examine the challenges that clear values and open communication aim to surmount, the strategies for embedding these principles into the organizational fabric, and the manifold benefits they unleash for both the employees and the organization at large.

At the core of every healthy business culture lie clear, shared values that encapsulate the essence of the company's mission and vision. These values act as a guiding star, providing direction and purpose to the organization's endeavors. They are instrumental in shaping the behaviors and attitudes of the workforce, ensuring that every action and decision aligns with the organization's goals. The process of defining these values requires thoughtful consideration and engagement from leadership, ensuring they are not only reflective of the company's aspirations but also resonate with the employees.

Open communication is the thread that weaves together the fabric of a healthy corporate culture. It establishes a platform for the free exchange of ideas, feedback, and concerns, thereby fostering an environment of trust and transparency. Open communication encourages collaboration and innovation, breaking down silos and creating a cohesive, unified workforce. It enables employees to voice their thoughts and suggestions, contributing to the continuous improvement and growth of the organization.

111

Implementing clear values and fostering open communication are not without their challenges. Organizations often grapple with ensuring the consistent application and reinforcement of these values across all levels. Similarly, creating a culture of open communication can be daunting, particularly in traditional hierarchical structures where information flow is typically top-down. This chapter will delve into these challenges, offering insights into how organizations can overcome them to build a thriving and inclusive culture.

The benefits of establishing clear values and fostering open communication are manifold. They include enhanced employee engagement and loyalty, improved decision-making, increased innovation, and a stronger alignment with the organization's strategic goals. A healthy business culture, underpinned by these elements, not only elevates employee satisfaction and performance but also significantly contributes to the organization's resilience and adaptability in the face of change.

As we embark on this exploration, it becomes evident that the cultivation of a healthy business culture, rooted in clear values and open communication, is a strategic imperative for organizations aiming for long-term success. These foundational elements serve as the catalyst for creating an environment where employees are engaged, motivated, and aligned with the company's mission and vision. Through the pages of this chapter, we will dissect the

112

intricacies of building such a culture, the obstacles that may arise, and the strategies to navigate these challenges, ultimately unlocking the full potential of the organization and its people.

Establishing Clear Values

The establishment of clear core values within an organization is not merely a statement of ethical intent; it is a foundational strategy that shapes the culture, guides decision-making, and influences every facet of organizational life. Core values act as an ethical compass, guiding the behavior of its members towards a unified direction aligned with the company's mission and vision. This essay delves into the significance of defining core values, their impact on decision-making, the enhancement of employee engagement, and the molding of corporate identity, underscoring their pivotal role in achieving organizational goals.

Core values are the essence of an organization's identity, embodying its principles, beliefs, and philosophies. They serve as a guiding light for behavior, decision-making, and the development of strategies and policies. The importance of defining these values lies in their ability to

113

provide a clear standard for what is deemed important within the organization. When values are well-defined, they create a sense of purpose and direction, offering employees a framework within which they can operate with a clear understanding of organizational expectations.

One of the primary roles of core values is to guide decision-making at all levels of the organization. In the complex and dynamic environment of modern business, decision-making can be fraught with ambiguity and ethical dilemmas. Core values offer a touchstone for decision-making, ensuring that choices are aligned with the organization's ethical standards and long-term objectives. This alignment reduces the risk of ethical breaches and enhances the consistency and quality of decisions made across the organization, fostering a culture of integrity and ethical conduct.

The integration of core values into the fabric of organizational life has a profound impact on employee engagement. When employees understand and align with the organization's core values, they are more likely to feel a sense of belonging and commitment to the company. This alignment fosters a deeper engagement with their work and

114

the organization's mission, driving motivation and satisfaction. Furthermore, when employees see their values reflected in the organization's actions, it reinforces their trust in the company, strengthening their emotional and psychological commitment.

Core values are integral to the formation and expression of corporate identity. They communicate to internal and external stakeholders what the organization stands for, its priorities, and how it distinguishes itself from competitors. A well-defined set of core values contributes to a strong and coherent corporate identity, enhancing the organization's reputation and brand image. This clarity in corporate identity attracts customers, investors, and employees who share similar values, fostering relationships based on mutual understanding and respect.

The true power of core values lies in their genuine integration into all aspects of the organization. This integration requires more than just stating values; it demands their embodiment in policies, practices, leadership behavior, and daily operations. Leaders play a crucial role in this process, modeling the values through their actions and decisions, and embedding them into the organizational culture. Additionally, recognizing and rewarding behaviors that align with core values reinforces their importance, encouraging their adoption throughout the organization.

Despite the clear benefits of establishing core values, organizations may face challenges in defining and implementing them effectively. These challenges include ensuring authenticity in the values chosen, achieving buy-in from all members of the organization, and maintaining the relevance of values over time. Overcoming these challenges requires a commitment to ongoing dialogue, reflection, and adaptation, ensuring that core values remain aligned with the evolving goals and realities of the organization.

The establishment of clear core values is a strategic imperative for organizations aiming to foster a culture of integrity, enhance decision-making, and engage employees. These values serve as an ethical compass, guiding behavior and strategies in alignment with the organization's mission and vision. By genuinely integrating core values into every facet of organizational life, leaders can mold a strong corporate identity, attract like-minded stakeholders, and build a foundation for long-term success. Despite the challenges in defining and implementing core values, their importance in achieving organizational goals and shaping corporate culture cannot be overstated. Through a commitment to living these values, organizations can navigate the complexities of the modern business landscape with integrity and purpose.

Reflective Leadership and the Genesis of Values

The journey of establishing organizational values commences with a period of reflection among the leadership team. This reflective process is pivotal, as it requires leaders to introspectively consider what the organization stands for beyond mere financial profitability. It involves deep discussions about the organization's purpose, its raison d'être, and the principles it seeks to embody. Leaders are tasked with envisioning the legacy they aim to create, considering the impact of their organization on its customers, employees, the community, and the environment. This phase is crucial for aligning the leadership team around a core set of beliefs that will guide the organization's future actions and decisions.

Following the reflective phase, the next step in establishing clear values involves the articulation of these principles into a set of core values. This process is iterative and collaborative, often involving input from various stakeholders within the organization to ensure the values are representative and inclusive. The defined values should be succinct, memorable, and resonate with all members of the organization. They need to reflect the unique identity of the organization, differentiating it from competitors while encapsulating its mission and vision. The articulation of these values is not merely about crafting statements but about capturing the essence of the organization's ethos.

Once the core values are defined, the critical task of communicating these values ensues. Effective communication is key to ensuring that the values are understood, embraced, and lived by everyone within the organization. This involves more than just listing values on the company website or in marketing materials; it requires a strategic and ongoing effort to embed these values in the consciousness of every employee. Leaders must utilize multiple channels and methods to communicate the values, including company-wide meetings, training sessions, internal communications, and through the example set by their own behavior. The goal is to make the values a living, breathing part of the organization's culture.

The true test of established values lies in their integration into every aspect of the organization. This integration requires a deliberate effort to weave the values into the fabric of the company through policies, practices, and daily operations. From the hiring process and performance evaluations to decision-making frameworks and customer interactions, the core values should serve as a guiding light. This integration ensures that the values are not just aspirational statements but are reflected in the tangible actions and behaviors of the organization. It also involves regular assessment and reinforcement of the values to ensure they remain relevant and are upheld over time.

Despite the best intentions, the process of establishing values can encounter several challenges. These include ensuring the authenticity of the values, achieving buy-in from all levels of the organization, and maintaining the relevance of the values in a changing business landscape. Overcoming these challenges requires transparency, open dialogue, and a commitment to embedding the values in organizational processes. Leaders must be prepared to listen, adapt, and lead by example to foster a culture that truly reflects the established values.

The process of establishing clear values within an organization is a comprehensive and reflective journey that lays the groundwork for its culture, decision-making, and stakeholder interactions. It starts with reflective leadership and moves through defining, communicating, and integrating these values into the organizational fabric. While challenges may arise, the benefits of having well-defined and integrated values—such as enhanced decision-making, employee engagement, and a strong corporate identity—are immeasurable. Ultimately, the effort to establish and uphold clear values is a testament to an organization's commitment to its foundational principles, guiding it towards achieving its mission and leaving a lasting impact on the world.

Aligning Employees To The Core Values

Aligning employees with organizational values is a strategic endeavor that underpins the creation of a cohesive and productive workplace culture. This alignment ensures that the behavior and decisions of employees resonate with the core principles of the organization, fostering an environment where shared values catalyze collective success.

120

Achieving this alignment involves a multifaceted approach that integrates value-centric hiring practices, comprehensive training programs, and recognition systems designed to reinforce desired behaviors.

The foundation of aligning employees with organizational values lies in the recruitment process. Value-centric hiring practices involve more than assessing a candidate's skills and experience; they require a deep dive into the individual's personal values and their compatibility with the organization's core principles. This alignment is crucial for ensuring that new hires are not only capable of performing their roles but are also predisposed to embody the company's values in their actions and decisions. Implementing value-centric hiring practices may include incorporating value-based questions into interviews, developing assessments that gauge value alignment, and involving multiple team members in the hiring process to ensure a comprehensive evaluation of the candidate's fit with the organizational culture.

Once employees are onboarded, training programs play a pivotal role in further aligning them with the organization's values. These programs should extend beyond skill and competency development to include comprehensive education on the company's mission, vision, and core principles. Effective training programs leverage interactive and engaging methodologies to immerse employees in the organization's values, facilitating a deeper understanding and internalization of these principles. Topics might cover ethical decision-making, teamwork and collaboration, customer service excellence, and other areas directly related to the organization's values. By embedding values into the fabric of training programs, organizations can ensure that employees not only comprehend these principles but are also equipped to apply them in their daily work.

Recognition systems are a powerful tool for reinforcing organizational values and encouraging behaviors that exemplify these principles. By acknowledging and rewarding employees who demonstrate a commitment to the organization's values, leaders can reinforce the importance of these principles and motivate others to emulate such behaviors. Recognition can take many forms, from formal awards and public acknowledgments to informal expressions of appreciation and team celebrations. The key is to ensure that the criteria for recognition are clearly tied to the demonstration of organizational values, making the link between values and rewarded behaviors explicit. This approach not only boosts morale but also strengthens the culture of values alignment across the organization.

The ultimate goal of aligning employees with organizational values is to foster a deep connection between the individual and the company. When employees genuinely share the organization's values, they are more likely to experience a sense of belonging and purpose, driving their motivation and commitment. This connection transcends the transactional aspects of employment, engendering a sense of loyalty and dedication that contributes to both individual fulfillment and organizational success. Employees who feel aligned with their company's values are more engaged, productive, and resilient, making them invaluable assets in the pursuit of organizational objectives.

Achieving alignment between employees and organizational values is not without its challenges. Diverse workforces may bring a wide array of personal values, making universal alignment difficult. Additionally, changes in leadership, strategy, or external conditions may necessitate a reevaluation of organizational values, posing challenges to maintaining alignment. To navigate these challenges,

123

organizations must commit to ongoing communication about values, provide continuous opportunities for value-related training and development, and adapt recognition systems to reflect evolving values and behaviors. Open dialogue about values, regular feedback mechanisms, and leadership's commitment to modeling values in action are critical for sustaining alignment and fostering a culture where organizational values are lived daily.

Aligning employees with organizational values is a complex yet rewarding process that enhances workplace culture, drives employee motivation, and contributes to the achievement of organizational goals. Through value-centric hiring practices, comprehensive training programs, and recognition systems that reward value-exemplifying behaviors, organizations can foster a deep connection between employees and the company's mission and purpose. While challenges may arise, a steadfast commitment to promoting and reinforcing organizational values will ensure that employees are not only aligned with but also deeply committed to the principles that define the organization. This alignment is essential for building a cohesive, motivated, and values-driven workforce poised for success in the dynamic landscape of modern business.

Fostering open communication within an organization is a critical component of cultivating a healthy business culture. This approach to communication serves as the cornerstone for a transparent, inclusive, and dynamic work environment, where the free exchange of ideas, feedback, and concerns is not only encouraged but valued. Open communication stands as a lifeline for organizations aiming to navigate the complexities of the modern business landscape, enabling them to address challenges proactively, innovate continuously, and foster a sense of unity and belonging among employees.

The culture of a business significantly influences its success, affecting everything from employee satisfaction and retention to productivity and profitability. Open communication plays a pivotal role in shaping this culture, creating an atmosphere of trust and respect. When leaders prioritize transparency and actively encourage the sharing of ideas and opinions, they signal to employees that their contributions are valued. This not only boosts morale but also enhances employees' sense of ownership and commitment to the organization's goals. Furthermore, open communication fosters diversity and inclusion by ensuring all voices are heard and considered, enriching the decision-making process with a multitude of perspectives.

Open communication is indispensable for effective problem-solving and innovation. In environments where employees feel comfortable voicing their ideas and concerns without fear of judgment or reprisal, organizations can identify and address issues before they escalate. This proactive approach to problem-solving saves resources and avoids the potential negative impacts of unresolved issues on morale and productivity. Moreover, a culture that encourages open dialogue is ripe for innovation. Employees who are free to express their thoughts and collaborate with colleagues are more likely to generate creative solutions and breakthrough ideas, driving the organization forward in its pursuit of excellence and competitive advantage.

The benefits of open communication extend beyond problem-solving and innovation to the very heart of the organization's social fabric. By fostering a culture of openness, leaders can cultivate a strong sense of community among employees. This sense of belonging is crucial for employee engagement and satisfaction, as individuals feel connected to their peers and aligned with the organization's values and objectives. A strong community within the workplace can act as a support system, helping employees navigate challenges and celebrate successes together, further reinforcing their commitment to the organization.

Fostering open communication requires intentional effort and strategic initiatives. Leaders can adopt several practices to encourage openness, including:

- Creating Multiple Channels for Dialogue: Organizations should provide various platforms for communication, such as regular team meetings, one-on-one check-ins, suggestion boxes, and digital forums. This ensures that employees have multiple avenues to express their ideas and feedback.
- Modeling Open Communication: Leadership plays a crucial role in setting the tone for open communication. Leaders should model this behavior by sharing information transparently, soliciting feedback, and demonstrating active listening. By leading by example, they can encourage employees to engage in open dialogue.

- Encouraging Diverse Perspectives: A culture of open communication embraces diversity, recognizing that innovation and problem-solving benefit from a range of perspectives. Leaders should encourage employees from different backgrounds, departments, and levels of the organization to share their insights, fostering an inclusive environment.

- Training and Support: Providing training on effective communication skills can empower employees to express their ideas and feedback constructively. Additionally, offering support and resources to facilitate open dialogue can remove barriers to communication, such as fear of negative consequences or lack of confidence.

- Recognizing and Rewarding Open Communication: Acknowledging and rewarding employees who actively participate in open dialogue can reinforce the value of communication. Recognition can take various forms, from verbal acknowledgment in meetings to awards for innovative ideas or constructive feedback.

Open communication is a vital component of a healthy business culture, underpinning the organization's ability to solve problems, innovate, and foster a strong sense of community. By prioritizing transparency, encouraging diverse perspectives, and implementing strategic initiatives to facilitate dialogue, leaders can cultivate an environment where open communication thrives. This not only enhances the organizational culture but also contributes to the overall success and sustainability of the business. Fostering open communication is, therefore, not just a leadership responsibility but a strategic imperative for organizations aiming to navigate the challenges of the modern business environment and achieve long-term success.

Creating Channels For Two-Way Communication

Fostering open communication within an organization is a vital strategy for building a transparent, inclusive, and collaborative work environment. Effective two-way communication facilitates a dialogue between employees and leadership, promoting a culture where feedback, ideas, and concerns are freely exchanged. Creating channels for this type of communication is not incidental; it requires deliberate planning and the implementation of intentional structures and practices that encourage openness and dialogue. Here we will discuss the significance of establishing channels for two-way communication, such as open-door policies, regular town hall meetings, and anonymous feedback tools, and how they contribute to fostering a culture of transparency and dialogue.

An open-door policy is more than a symbolic gesture; it's a commitment from leadership to be accessible and available to employees. This policy encourages employees to approach leaders with their ideas, concerns, and feedback, knowing they will be heard and valued. The effectiveness of an open-door policy lies in its ability to break down hierarchical barriers, making leaders more approachable and fostering a sense of mutual respect and trust. For this policy to be successful, leaders must actively demonstrate their willingness to listen and engage with employees, ensuring that this practice translates into meaningful interactions rather than remaining a mere statement of intent.

Town hall meetings are a powerful platform for enhancing two-way communication within an organization. These gatherings provide an opportunity for leadership to share company updates, strategic directions, and successes, fostering a sense of unity and purpose among employees. Equally important, they offer a forum for employees to voice their opinions, ask questions, and discuss challenges in an open and supportive environment. Regular scheduling of town hall meetings demonstrates an ongoing commitment to transparency and ensures that communication flows consistently in both directions. To maximize their impact, these meetings should be structured to encourage active participation from employees across all levels of the organization.

While open-door policies and town hall meetings encourage direct interaction, anonymous feedback tools offer an alternative channel for employees who may feel uncomfortable expressing their concerns openly. These tools provide a safe space for employees to share honest feedback without fear of retaliation or judgment. Implementing anonymous feedback mechanisms, such as suggestion boxes or digital platforms, signals an organization's genuine interest in hearing all voices, including those that might otherwise remain silent. For anonymous feedback to be effective, it is crucial that leadership respond to the feedback received, either by addressing specific issues or by communicating how the input is being used to inform decisions and

131

improvements. This responsiveness reinforces the value placed on employee input and encourages continued engagement.

The establishment of channels for two-way communication has a profound impact on organizational culture. By promoting openness and dialogue, these channels contribute to building a transparent work environment where employees feel valued and engaged. This openness not only enhances problem-solving and innovation by leveraging diverse perspectives but also builds trust between employees and leadership. Furthermore, effective two-way communication plays a crucial role in conflict resolution, allowing for issues to be addressed constructively and collaboratively before they escalate.

To enhance two-way communication, organizations must go beyond simply establishing channels; they must actively promote and support their use. This can involve training leaders in active listening and communication skills, regularly promoting the availability of these channels to employees, and creating incentives for meaningful participation. Additionally, organizations should regularly assess the effectiveness of their communication channels,

132

seeking feedback from employees on how they can be improved and adapting strategies based on this input.

Creating channels for two-way communication is essential for fostering an open communication culture within organizations. An open-door policy, regular town hall meetings, and anonymous feedback tools are critical components of a comprehensive communication strategy that values employee input and promotes transparency. By implementing and actively supporting these channels, organizations can enhance dialogue, build trust, and encourage a culture of openness and collaboration. Effective two-way communication is not just about sharing information; it's about creating a participatory environment where every voice is heard and valued, contributing to the overall success and cohesion of the organization.

Barriers to Open Communication

Fostering open communication within an organization is essential for its growth, innovation, and the well-being of its employees. However, achieving this level of openness is often challenged by various barriers that can stem from the organization's structure, culture, and practices. These barriers can intimidate employees from speaking up, create mistrust, and discourage dissent, ultimately stifling the free flow of ideas and feedback. Overcoming these obstacles is crucial for establishing a culture where open communication is not only encouraged but also practiced.

One of the most significant barriers to open communication is the presence of rigid hierarchical structures within an organization. These structures can create an environment where employees feel intimidated by the prospect of speaking up, especially when their feedback or ideas challenge the status quo or the opinions of those in higher positions. This intimidation can lead to self-censorship, where employees withhold valuable insights out of fear of repercussions.

Another barrier is the lack of trust in the confidentiality and impact of sharing feedback. Employees may fear that their feedback will not be kept confidential or that it will not lead to any meaningful change. This mistrust can stem from past experiences where feedback was either mishandled or ignored, leading to a reluctance to engage in open communication.

Cultural norms within an organization can also discourage open communication, especially when dissent is viewed negatively. In cultures that prioritize harmony and consensus over healthy debate, employees may feel pressured to conform rather than express differing opinions. This pressure can suppress innovative ideas and prevent the organization from benefiting from diverse perspectives.

Leaders play a critical role in overcoming barriers to open communication by actively demonstrating the value of every employee's voice. This can be achieved by creating multiple channels for feedback, actively seeking input from employees at all levels, and acknowledging contributions in meaningful ways. Leaders should emphasize that all feedback, whether positive or negative, is welcomed and valued as a tool for improvement.

To address concerns about confidentiality and trust, leaders must ensure that mechanisms are in place for employees to share feedback anonymously. Tools such as anonymous surveys, suggestion boxes, or digital platforms can provide employees with a safe means of expressing their thoughts without fear of identification or retaliation. Additionally, establishing clear policies to protect employees who speak up from any form of reprisal is essential for building trust in the feedback process.

Perhaps the most crucial step in overcoming barriers to open communication is acting on the feedback received. When employees see that their input leads to tangible changes, it reinforces the effectiveness of open communication and encourages further participation. Leaders should communicate the actions taken in response to feedback, explaining how it has influenced decisions or led to improvements. This transparency not only demonstrates the value placed on employee input but also shows a commitment to continuous learning and development.

Overcoming barriers to open communication requires a concerted effort to cultivate a culture of openness and transparency. This involves more than just implementing policies; it requires a shift in mindset at all levels of the organization. Leaders must model open communication in their interactions, encouraging open dialogue, and showing vulnerability by sharing their own challenges and learning experiences. Training programs that focus on communication skills, active listening, and constructive feedback can also equip employees with the tools they need to engage in open and effective dialogue.

Creating an environment where dissent is not only tolerated but encouraged is vital for fostering innovation and critical thinking. Leaders should create forums for debate, encourage alternative viewpoints, and demonstrate how constructive dissent can lead to better outcomes. Recognizing and rewarding employees who challenge assumptions or propose new ideas can further encourage a culture where diverse perspectives are celebrated.

Overcoming barriers to open communication is essential for building a culture where ideas flourish, feedback leads to improvement, and employees feel valued and heard. By addressing the challenges posed by hierarchical structures, lack of trust, and cultural norms, leaders can pave the way for more transparent, inclusive, and dynamic communication practices. Through consistent effort, ensuring anonymity and protection, and acting on feedback, organizations can demonstrate the tangible benefits of open communication. Cultivating this environment requires not just structural changes but a commitment to fostering openness, trust, and respect at every level of the organization. In doing so,

137

organizations can unlock the full potential of their workforce, driving innovation, engagement, and success in an ever-evolving business landscape.

Benefits of Clear Values and Open Communication

When a company's values are clear and communication channels are open, decision-making becomes more streamlined and aligned with the organization's strategic goals. Leaders and employees alike can reference these core values when facing choices, ensuring decisions reinforce the desired culture and drive the company forward in a cohesive manner.

Understanding and aligning with the company's values can significantly boost employee engagement and motivation. Employees who see their work as part of a larger purpose are more likely to be committed and put in the extra effort. Open communication further enhances this effect by making employees feel respected and valued, knowing their opinions can influence change.

Open communication fosters a sense of community among employees, as it encourages sharing, collaboration, and mutual support. When employees feel they are part of a community that shares common values and goals, it strengthens their sense of belonging and loyalty to the organization.

A culture that values open communication is ripe for innovation. By encouraging the free exchange of ideas and feedback, organizations can tap into the collective creativity and knowledge of their workforce. This environment not only generates innovative solutions to internal challenges but also leads to the development of new products, services, and business models that keep the company competitive.

Implementing these cultural foundations requires a deliberate approach. Leadership must lead by example, demonstrating commitment to the organization's values and actively engaging in open communication. Training programs should reinforce these principles, and policies should be put in place to support their practice. Regular assessments of the company's culture can help identify areas for improvement, ensuring that the values remain relevant and communication channels effectively meet the needs of the organization.

In the complex and dynamic realm of modern business, the significance of establishing clear values and fostering open communication transcends mere advantageous practices; these are, in fact, the bedrock of a healthy corporate culture. This foundational duo acts as the architect of an environment where motivation flourishes, strategic objectives are seamlessly aligned, innovation is nurtured, and a profound sense of community binds the organization together. While the path to embedding these elements within the corporate fabric is fraught with challenges, the myriad benefits they yield in terms of enhancing employee engagement, bolstering operational effectiveness, and securing long-term organizational success are substantial and multifaceted.

Clear values serve as the compass that guides the organization through the complexities of the business world, ensuring that every decision and action is in harmony with the company's core mission and vision. By articulating what the organization stands for, leaders can cultivate a workforce that is not only motivated but also deeply aligned with the company's goals. This alignment fosters a culture of accountability, where employees are empowered to take ownership of their roles, driving forward with purpose and

140

precision. The establishment of clear values thus becomes a catalyst for strategic coherence, ensuring that the organization moves as a cohesive unit toward its objectives.

Similarly, open communication is the lifeblood of a thriving organizational culture, facilitating the free flow of ideas, feedback, and dialogue across all levels of the hierarchy. It creates a platform for collaboration and innovation, where diverse perspectives are valued and explored, leading to breakthroughs and creative solutions. Open communication also underpins a strong sense of community within the organization, fostering an environment of trust and mutual respect. In such a culture, employees feel heard and appreciated, contributing to higher levels of engagement and job satisfaction.

Implementing clear values and open communication is not without its hurdles. Challenges such as ensuring consistency in values across global operations, breaking down traditional communication barriers, and cultivating a genuine culture of openness require strategic effort and commitment. However, the endeavor to overcome these challenges is a worthwhile investment. Leadership commitment, continuous reinforcement, and the creation of channels that support

141

open dialogue are critical strategies that can facilitate the successful integration of these cultural components.

The benefits of establishing clear values and fostering open communication are manifold and extend far beyond immediate operational improvements. They are instrumental in building a motivated and cohesive workforce that is agile, innovative, and fully engaged in the pursuit of the organization's goals. Such a culture enhances operational effectiveness, driving productivity and efficiency while also laying the groundwork for long-term success. Moreover, in an era marked by rapid change and uncertainty, these cultural foundations equip organizations to navigate shifts in the market, technological advancements, and evolving customer expectations with resilience and adaptability.

In the contemporary business landscape, marked by its relentless pace and volatility, organizations that prioritize the cultivation of clear values and open communication are uniquely positioned to thrive. These cultural pillars attract and retain top talent, individuals who seek workplaces where they can connect with the company's purpose, grow professionally, and contribute to meaningful work. Furthermore, by driving sustainable growth through innovation and strategic alignment, companies can not only survive but flourish amidst change.

Establishing clear values and fostering open communication are indispensable practices that form the cornerstone of a healthy business culture. They are essential for creating an environment where employees are motivated, operations are aligned with strategic goals, innovation thrives, and a strong sense of community prevails. While challenges in implementing these elements are inevitable, the rewards — enhanced employee engagement, operational effectiveness, and enduring success — are profound. In the ever-evolving business environment, companies that lay these cultural foundations are well-equipped to navigate change, securing a competitive edge and achieving sustainable growth in the process.

Chapter 6: Facilitating Employee Development and Career Progression

In an era marked by rapid technological advancements and ever-shifting market dynamics, the strategic importance of facilitating employee development and career progression has never been more pronounced. This imperative reflects an organization's recognition of its workforce as its most invaluable asset and underscores a deep-rooted commitment to nurturing this human capital. The embodiment of this commitment is found in the implementation of comprehensive training and development programs, the availability of mentorship opportunities, and the cultivation of a workplace culture that champions continuous learning and professional growth. Such initiatives are not merely beneficial but are essential for equipping employees with the requisite skills and knowledge for their current roles while simultaneously preparing them for the impending challenges and opportunities that lie ahead.

Employee development is an encompassing term that includes a vast array of activities aimed at enhancing the skills, knowledge, and competencies of an organization's workforce. From targeted training sessions and workshops to mentorship programs and continuous learning platforms, the scope of employee development is broad and varied. This multifaceted approach ensures that employees are not only proficient in their current roles but are also well-prepared to take on future responsibilities and challenges. In doing so, organizations can foster a workforce that is adaptable, versatile, and ready to meet the demands of a rapidly evolving business landscape.

The contemporary business environment is characterized by its fast-paced and unpredictable nature, with technological innovations and market shifts occurring at a previously unseen velocity. In this context, the need for ongoing skill development and adaptability cannot be overstated. Organizations that place a premium on employee development find themselves at a distinct advantage, able to swiftly respond to change, drive innovation, and sustain a competitive edge. These organizations understand that investing in the development of their employees is tantamount to investing in their own future success.

Beyond the immediate benefits of enhanced skills and competencies, employee development initiatives serve as a powerful signal to the workforce of the organization's investment in their personal and professional growth. This signal fosters a profound sense of loyalty and engagement among employees, who perceive their employer's commitment to their development as a testament to their value within the organization. Such a perception

145

not only boosts morale and job satisfaction but also cultivates a culture of mutual respect and dedication, where employees are motivated to contribute their best efforts towards the organization's objectives.

The correlation between employee development and enhanced loyalty and engagement is well-documented. Employees who feel supported in their professional growth trajectories are more likely to exhibit a higher degree of commitment to their organization, displaying increased motivation, productivity, and a willingness to go above and beyond in their roles. This heightened level of engagement is a crucial driver of organizational performance, contributing to improved outcomes across various metrics, including innovation, customer satisfaction, and overall profitability.

Facilitating employee development and career progression is a strategic imperative that plays a critical role in an organization's success. By providing comprehensive training and development opportunities, fostering a culture of continuous learning, and offering mentorship and support, organizations can ensure their workforce is equipped to navigate the complexities of the modern business environment. This commitment to nurturing the growth of its people not only prepares the organization to face future challenges but also signals to employees that they are a valued and integral part of the company's vision for success. As such,

146

prioritizing employee development is not just a strategic necessity but a fundamental aspect of cultivating a resilient, innovative, and competitive organization.

The Significance of Employee Development

Employee development stands as a cornerstone of organizational strategy in the modern business landscape. It encompasses a comprehensive approach to enhancing the skills, knowledge, and competencies of the workforce, ensuring that employees are equipped to meet both current and future challenges. In an era marked by rapid technological advancements and shifting market dynamics, the continuous development of employees is not just beneficial but essential for organizational resilience and competitiveness.

The ability to adapt to changing circumstances is crucial for survival and success in today's business environment. Employee development plays a pivotal role in building this adaptability by ensuring that the workforce is proficient in the latest technologies, methodologies, and industry best practices. By investing in the ongoing development of employees, organizations can quickly pivot in response to new challenges, seize emerging opportunities, and mitigate potential risks. This agility is especially critical in industries subject to rapid technological change, where the skills required today may be obsolete tomorrow.

Innovation is the lifeblood of competitive advantage, and it is fueled by a skilled and knowledgeable workforce. Employee development initiatives that encourage creative thinking, problem-solving, and the exploration of new ideas can significantly enhance an organization's capacity for innovation. Training programs that focus on emerging technologies, design thinking, and innovation management equip employees with the tools they need to contribute novel solutions to complex problems. Furthermore, creating a culture that values learning and development can inspire employees to challenge the status quo and think outside the box, leading to breakthrough products, services, and processes.

In the fiercely competitive global market, the skills and competencies of an organization's workforce can be a key differentiator. Employee development ensures that an organization's human capital remains a step ahead,

148

possessing the advanced skills and knowledge required to outperform competitors. This competitive edge is not only about technical proficiency but also encompasses soft skills such as leadership, communication, and strategic thinking. By prioritizing comprehensive development programs that address both hard and soft skills, organizations can build a well-rounded, highly capable workforce poised to take on leadership roles in their respective industries.

Employee development initiatives signal to the workforce that the organization values their growth and is committed to their success. This investment in personal and professional development can significantly boost employee loyalty and engagement. When employees see that their employer is dedicated to supporting their career progression, they are more likely to feel a strong sense of commitment to the organization. This loyalty translates into higher levels of employee satisfaction, reduced turnover rates, and a more motivated workforce. Moreover, engaged employees who are actively developing their skills are likely to be more productive and contribute positively to the organization's culture and performance.

For employee development to be impactful, it must be strategic, continuous, and aligned with organizational goals. This requires a multifaceted approach, including:

- Tailored Training Programs: Developing customized training programs that address the specific needs of the workforce and the strategic objectives of the organization. This includes both on-the-job training and opportunities for formal education.
- Career Pathing: Working with employees to define clear career paths that align with their strengths, interests, and the needs of the organization. This helps employees visualize their future within the company and understand the steps needed to achieve their career goals.
- Mentorship and Coaching: Establishing mentorship and coaching programs that pair less experienced employees with seasoned professionals. These relationships can provide valuable guidance, feedback, and support for personal and professional development.
- Learning Culture: Cultivating a culture that values and encourages continuous learning. This can be achieved

by recognizing and rewarding development achievements, providing time and resources for learning, and encouraging knowledge sharing among employees.

The significance of employee development in the modern business environment cannot be overstated. By prioritizing the continuous growth and development of their workforce, organizations can enhance their adaptability, drive innovation, maintain a competitive edge, and foster employee loyalty and engagement. Effective employee development requires a strategic approach, tailored to the needs of the workforce and aligned with organizational objectives. Through comprehensive training programs, career pathing, mentorship, and a culture of continuous learning, organizations can unlock the full potential of their employees, ensuring long-term success and sustainability in the ever-evolving business landscape.

Impact of Training and Development Programs

Comprehensive training and development programs are indispensable components of a robust employee development strategy, pivotal for nurturing a workforce that is skilled, adaptable, and aligned with organizational goals. These programs serve a dual purpose: they not only enhance the current competencies of employees but also prepare them for future challenges and opportunities. In an era marked by rapid technological advancements and shifting market dynamics, the ability of an organization to remain competitive is closely tied to its commitment to continuous learning and development.

At the core of training and development programs is the enhancement of employees' technical proficiencies and soft skills. Technical skills training ensures that employees are adept in the job-specific tools and technologies critical to their roles, thereby increasing efficiency and productivity. This type of training is especially crucial in industries where technological competencies can significantly impact performance and outcomes.

Equally important is the development of soft skills, which include communication, leadership, problem-solving, and teamwork abilities. These skills are fundamental to fostering a collaborative work environment, enhancing decision-making, and facilitating effective leadership.

152

Programs designed to enhance soft skills contribute to building a more dynamic and cohesive workforce, capable of navigating the complexities of interpersonal interactions and leading with empathy and insight.

A forward-looking aspect of training and development programs is their focus on anticipating and preparing for future skill requirements. As industries evolve and new trends emerge, the demand for certain skills can shift dramatically. Organizations that proactively identify these future trends and incorporate relevant training into their development programs can position their workforce at the forefront of industry advancements. This proactive approach not only ensures the relevance of the workforce but also empowers employees to embrace change and innovation confidently.

Training and development programs are critical drivers of innovation and organizational excellence. By equipping employees with the latest skills and encouraging a culture of learning, organizations can foster an environment ripe for innovation. Employees who are continually learning are more likely to think creatively, challenge existing paradigms, and propose novel solutions to problems. Moreover, a workforce that is well-versed in the latest industry trends and

153

technologies can contribute to the development of cutting-edge products, services, and processes, thereby enhancing the organization's competitive edge.

The strategic implementation of training and development programs involves several key considerations. First, programs must be tailored to the specific needs of the organization and its employees. This requires a thorough assessment of current skill gaps, as well as an understanding of the organization's strategic objectives. Customizing training programs to address these needs ensures that learning initiatives are both relevant and impactful.

Second, the delivery of training programs should leverage diverse methodologies to accommodate different learning styles. This can include a blend of traditional classroom training, online learning modules, on-the-job training, and experiential learning opportunities. Such a multifaceted approach can enhance engagement and retention of knowledge.

Third, organizations should establish metrics to evaluate the effectiveness of training and development programs. This can involve assessing improvements in performance, productivity, and employee satisfaction following training initiatives. By measuring outcomes, organizations can refine their training programs to maximize their impact.

Beyond the implementation of specific training programs, fostering a culture of continuous learning is essential for sustaining the long-term impact of employee development initiatives. This culture encourages employees to take ownership of their learning journeys, seek out opportunities for growth, and share knowledge with their peers. Organizations can support this culture by providing access to learning resources, recognizing and rewarding learning achievements, and creating pathways for career advancement that are linked to ongoing development.

Training and development programs are foundational to the strategic growth and sustainability of organizations. By enhancing technical and soft skills, anticipating future skill requirements, and driving innovation, these programs play a critical role in maintaining a workforce that is skilled, adaptable, and aligned with organizational goals. The strategic implementation of these programs, coupled with a commitment to fostering a culture of continuous learning, can ensure that organizations not only meet the challenges of today but are also poised to seize the opportunities of tomorrow. In doing so, they invest not just in the development of their employees but in the future success and excellence of the organization as a whole.

.

The Role of Mentorship in Career Progression

Mentorship programs play a crucial role in facilitating employee career progression. By pairing employees with experienced mentors, organizations can provide valuable guidance, support, and insights that are instrumental in navigating career paths and overcoming professional challenges. Mentorship fosters a culture of learning and knowledge sharing, where employees can benefit from the experiences and wisdom of their colleagues. This personalized approach to development not only accelerates career growth but also strengthens the organization's talent pipeline, ensuring that there is a ready pool of skilled individuals prepared to step into leadership roles.

Mentorship programs are a cornerstone of effective organizational development, serving as a vital conduit for the transfer of knowledge, skills, and professional insights. These programs significantly impact employee career progression by pairing less experienced employees with seasoned professionals who can offer guidance, support, and invaluable insights.

Mentorship is instrumental in cultivating a culture of continuous learning and knowledge sharing within an organization. This culture is characterized by an open exchange of ideas, experiences, and challenges, where learning from one another is highly valued. Through mentorship, experienced professionals share their wisdom and insights, providing mentees with a broader understanding of their field, the organization, and the industry at large. This exchange not only benefits the mentee but also offers mentors the opportunity to refine their leadership and communication skills, creating a mutually beneficial learning environment. Such a culture encourages employees to remain curious, seek out new knowledge, and continuously develop their skills, fostering an atmosphere where innovation and growth thrive.

Mentorship is a powerful tool for accelerating career growth. Mentors provide personalized advice and support, helping mentees navigate the complexities of their career paths. This guidance can include everything from developing specific skills to understanding organizational politics and identifying career advancement opportunities. By leveraging their mentors' experiences, mentees can make more informed decisions about their professional development and career trajectory. This personalized approach to career progression enables employees to achieve their career goals more efficiently and effectively, contributing to higher levels of job satisfaction and engagement.

Implementing mentorship programs is a strategic investment in an organization's future. These programs play a critical role in identifying and developing high-potential employees who are capable of stepping into leadership roles. Through mentorship, employees gain the skills, knowledge, and confidence needed to take on greater responsibilities. This process not only prepares individuals for leadership positions but also ensures that the organization has a robust talent pipeline ready to meet future challenges. As mentors guide their mentees through the intricacies of leadership and management, they contribute to building a reservoir of skilled individuals who are prepared to lead the organization toward its strategic objectives.

Mentorship is essential for nurturing future leaders within an organization. By providing emerging leaders with role models, mentors offer a blueprint for effective leadership. Mentees observe firsthand the qualities that define successful leaders, such as decision-making ability, strategic thinking, empathy, and resilience. Furthermore, mentorship provides a safe space for mentees to discuss leadership challenges, explore different leadership styles, and receive constructive feedback on their approach. This hands-on learning experience is invaluable for preparing the next generation of leaders, ensuring that they are equipped with the necessary competencies and mindset to lead successfully.

For mentorship programs to be effective, organizations must carefully design and implement these initiatives. This involves matching mentors and mentees based on complementary skills, interests, and career goals; providing training for mentors on how to effectively guide and support their mentees; and establishing clear objectives and expectations for the mentorship relationship. Regular check-ins and feedback sessions can help monitor the progress of the mentorship, ensuring that it remains aligned with the goals of both the mentee and the organization. Additionally, recognizing and celebrating the successes of mentorship pairs can reinforce the value of the program and encourage ongoing participation.

Mentorship plays a pivotal role in facilitating employee career progression, fostering a culture of learning, accelerating individual growth, and strengthening the organization's talent pipeline. By providing employees with access to experienced mentors, organizations can equip their workforce with the skills, knowledge, and insights needed to navigate their careers successfully. Moreover, mentorship programs are critical for identifying and nurturing future leaders, ensuring that the organization is prepared to meet the challenges of tomorrow. Implementing effective mentorship programs requires thoughtful planning, commitment, and support from leadership, but the benefits—enhanced employee development, increased job satisfaction, and a robust talent pipeline—far outweigh the investment, contributing to the long-term success and sustainability of the organization.

Creating a culture that values and encourages continuous learning is essential for maximizing the benefits of employee development initiatives. Organizations can foster such a culture by recognizing and rewarding learning achievements, providing access to learning resources and platforms, and encouraging employees to set and pursue personal development goals. Additionally, leaders should model a commitment to continuous learning by engaging in development activities themselves and sharing their learning experiences with their teams. This culture of continuous learning ensures that the organization and its employees remain agile, adaptable, and prepared for the future.

Fostering a culture of continuous learning within an organization is a strategic imperative in today's fast-paced and ever-evolving business environment. Such a culture not only enhances the skill set of the workforce but also ensures organizational agility, adaptability, and long-term sustainability. Creating an ecosystem where continuous learning is valued and promoted involves a multifaceted approach, integrating the recognition of learning achievements, providing access to diverse learning resources,

161

and setting a tone at the top that prioritizes personal and professional growth.

One of the foundational steps in fostering a culture of continuous learning is the recognition and reward of learning achievements. Acknowledging employees' efforts to develop new skills or enhance existing ones demonstrates the organization's commitment to their growth. This recognition can take various forms, from formal awards and certifications to informal acknowledgments in team meetings or through internal communication channels. Rewards for learning achievements not only motivate the individual learner but also serve as an inspiration to their peers, reinforcing the value placed on continuous personal development.

Equipping employees with the tools and resources necessary for continuous learning is crucial. This involves providing access to a variety of learning platforms, such as online courses, workshops, seminars, and conferences that cater to diverse learning needs and preferences. Organizations should also consider creating internal knowledge-sharing platforms where employees can exchange insights, experiences, and best practices. By diversifying the learning resources available, organizations can accommodate different learning styles and schedules, making learning more accessible and engaging for everyone.

A culture of continuous learning thrives when employees are encouraged to set and pursue personal development goals. Organizations can facilitate this by incorporating personal development planning into the performance review process, allowing employees to identify their learning objectives and align them with their career aspirations and organizational goals. Providing employees with the time and resources to achieve these goals is essential, as it underscores the organization's support for their professional growth. Moreover, regular check-ins on the progress of these goals ensure accountability and offer opportunities for feedback and adjustment.

Leadership plays a pivotal role in cultivating a culture of continuous learning. When leaders actively engage in their own development and openly share their learning experiences with their teams, they set a powerful example. This modeling behavior demonstrates that learning is a priority at all levels of the organization and is integral to professional success. Leaders should also be proactive in facilitating learning opportunities for their teams, whether by mentoring, coaching, or providing access to learning resources. By embodying the principles of continuous learning, leaders can inspire their teams to embrace a similar commitment to personal and professional development.

Beyond individual initiatives, fostering a culture of continuous learning requires the creation of a supportive learning environment. This environment is characterized by psychological safety, where employees feel comfortable taking risks, asking questions, and admitting mistakes without fear of reprisal. Encouraging experimentation and viewing failures as learning opportunities are key aspects of such an environment. Additionally, fostering cross-functional collaboration and team learning initiatives can enhance the collective knowledge base of the organization, contributing to a more dynamic and innovative culture.

While the benefits of fostering a culture of continuous learning are clear, organizations may face challenges in its implementation, such as resource constraints, resistance to change, and difficulties in measuring the impact of learning initiatives. Overcoming these challenges requires a strategic approach that prioritizes learning as a core organizational value, secures buy-in from all levels of the organization, and implements effective metrics to track learning outcomes and their impact on performance.

Fostering a culture of continuous learning is a strategic necessity in the modern business landscape. By recognizing and rewarding learning achievements, providing access to diverse learning resources, encouraging personal development goals, and modeling a commitment to continuous learning at the leadership level, organizations can ensure their workforce remains agile, adaptable, and prepared for future challenges. This culture of learning not only enhances employee development and organizational competitiveness but also nurtures an engaged, motivated, and innovative workforce committed to driving the organization forward.

Adaptability and Continuous Learning

The only constant in business is change. A healthy business culture is one that embraces adaptability and fosters a mindset of continuous learning among its workforce. Companies that encourage innovation and are open to new ideas can quickly adapt to market changes and technological advancements. This involves not only investing in employee training and development but also creating a safe environment for experimentation and failure. By viewing mistakes as learning opportunities, companies can cultivate a culture of resilience and agility.

Furthermore, continuous learning extends beyond professional development to include learning from diverse perspectives and backgrounds. Inclusive cultures that value diversity are better positioned to innovate and meet the needs of a global customer base. Thus, promoting diversity, equity, and inclusion should be an integral part of a company's cultural fabric.

While the benefits of facilitating employee development are clear, organizations may face challenges in implementing effective development strategies. These challenges can include budgetary constraints, identifying relevant training needs, and measuring the impact of development initiatives. To overcome these challenges, organizations must prioritize employee development within their strategic planning, employ innovative and cost-effective training solutions, and establish metrics to evaluate the effectiveness of development programs. By addressing these challenges proactively, organizations can ensure that their employee development initiatives are impactful, sustainable, and aligned with both individual and organizational goals.

The strategic imperative of facilitating employee development and career progression holds transformative potential for both organizational success and employee fulfillment. This commitment, manifested through the delivery of comprehensive training and development programs, the provision of mentorship opportunities, and the cultivation of a culture steeped in continuous learning, empowers organizations to arm their workforce with the essential skills and knowledge required to not only excel in their current roles but also to navigate the evolving challenges of the future. Such an investment in the growth and development of employees transcends mere operational enhancements; it is a pivotal driver of organizational performance, innovation, and competitiveness, positioning the company favorably within the ever-competitive business landscape.

Investing in employee development is intrinsically linked to enhanced organizational performance. By ensuring that employees are well-equipped with up-to-date skills and comprehensive industry knowledge, organizations can significantly improve productivity, efficiency, and innovation. This constant elevation of employee capabilities enables companies to stay at the forefront of technological advancements and market trends, ensuring they remain competitive and agile in a fast-paced business environment. Moreover, such strategic investment in human capital is essential for fostering a culture of excellence and high performance, where continuous improvement and the pursuit of excellence are inherent values.

Beyond the tangible benefits of improved performance and competitiveness, prioritizing employee development has a profound impact on employee engagement and loyalty. When organizations invest in their employees' growth, they convey a powerful message of value and trust, significantly enhancing job satisfaction and morale. This sense of being valued and invested in fosters a deep-seated loyalty among employees, translating into higher levels of engagement, reduced turnover rates, and a greater willingness to go above and beyond in their roles. Engaged employees are the cornerstone of a vibrant and dynamic organizational culture, one that is resilient in the face of challenges and adaptable to change.

The benefits of facilitating employee development reverberate throughout the organization, contributing to the cultivation of a resilient, dynamic, and innovative culture. In such an environment, continuous learning is celebrated, and employees are encouraged to explore new ideas, take calculated risks, and contribute creatively to the organization's goals. This culture of resilience and dynamism is invaluable in navigating the complexities and uncertainties of the business world, enabling organizations to thrive amidst change and uncertainty.

By prioritizing employee development, organizations signal a profound commitment not only to their immediate operational goals but also to their long-term success. This strategic focus on nurturing and developing human capital is indicative of a forward-thinking organization that recognizes the importance of preparing its workforce for the future. It lays a solid foundation for sustained achievement and growth, ensuring that the organization and its employees are well-positioned to seize new opportunities and tackle emerging challenges head-on.

The strategic imperative of facilitating employee development and career progression is a multifaceted endeavor with far-reaching implications for both organizational success and employee satisfaction. Through targeted investments in training and development, mentorship, and the cultivation of a culture that values continuous learning, organizations can significantly enhance their performance, competitiveness, and adaptability. Moreover, this commitment to employee growth fosters a culture of engagement, loyalty, and resilience, laying the groundwork for a vibrant and dynamic organizational environment. Ultimately, prioritizing employee development is a clear demonstration of an organization's dedication to its people and its future, serving as a cornerstone for enduring success and growth in an ever-evolving business landscape.

Chapter 7: Recognition and Empowerment

In the intricate tapestry of corporate culture, the threads of recognition and empowerment weave a pattern of positivity, engagement, and mutual respect that defines the essence of a thriving organization. Recognizing and rewarding employees for their contributions stand as pivotal practices that significantly uplift morale, foster a culture of excellence, and encourage every member of the organization to aspire towards higher achievements. Timely, specific recognition that resonates with the company's core values acts as a powerful motivator, reinforcing desired behaviors and outcomes. This recognition can manifest in myriad forms, from formal award programs that celebrate significant accomplishments to the simplicity of informal shout-outs or personalized notes of appreciation during team meetings. Such gestures of acknowledgment not only validate the individual's efforts but also serve as a beacon of inspiration for others.

Equally imperative to the cultivation of a positive corporate culture is the empowerment of employees, enabling them to take ownership of their work and make impactful decisions. This sense of trust and value, when instilled within the workforce, significantly heightens their engagement and dedication to their roles. Empowerment transcends the mere delegation of tasks; it involves providing employees with opportunities for professional growth, granting autonomy in task execution, and inviting their participation in decision-making processes that bear on their work and the broader organizational objectives. Such empowerment not only enhances job satisfaction but also fosters a sense of agency among employees, driving them to invest more fully in their work and the success of the organization.

The symbiotic relationship between recognition and empowerment forms the cornerstone of a vibrant corporate culture, one that champions engagement, stimulates motivation, and nurtures a profound sense of belonging among employees. These practices do more than just celebrate individual milestones or delegate authority; they lay the groundwork for a dynamic organizational environment where innovation is kindled, loyalty is deepened, and a

172

collective pursuit of excellence is vigorously upheld. The interplay between recognizing achievements and empowering employees to take initiative underpins a culture where every individual feels valued and inspired to contribute their best towards the collective goals of the organization.

In fostering such a culture, organizations unlock the potential for transformative growth, both at the individual and corporate levels. Recognition and empowerment, therefore, are not merely beneficial practices but essential elements in the strategic development of a corporate culture that excels in engaging its workforce, driving innovation, and maintaining a competitive edge in the ever-evolving business landscape. This chapter will delve deeper into the mechanisms of effective recognition and empowerment, exploring how these practices can be strategically implemented to foster an environment where employees feel genuinely appreciated and empowered, thus contributing to the overall success and vibrancy of the corporate culture.

The Importance of Employee Recognition

Employee recognition is a vital tool in enhancing morale and fostering a culture of appreciation within an organization. It serves multiple purposes: validating the individual's contributions, reinforcing the behaviors and achievements that drive the company forward, and setting a benchmark of excellence for others to aspire to. Recognition, when executed effectively, transcends mere acknowledgment; it becomes a powerful motivator, encouraging employees to exceed their own expectations and strive for higher standards of performance.

Employee recognition stands as a pivotal component within the organizational framework, significantly impacting morale and cultivating an environment where appreciation and acknowledgment flourish. This strategic tool does more than merely acknowledge individual efforts; it serves to validate contributions, reinforce desirable behaviors and accomplishments, and establish benchmarks of excellence. When thoughtfully and effectively implemented, recognition evolves beyond simple acknowledgment, transforming into a profound motivator that propels employees to surpass their benchmarks and aim for elevated standards of achievement.

174

The impact of employee recognition on morale cannot be overstated. Acknowledging the hard work and achievements of employees sends a clear message that their efforts are noticed and valued. This acknowledgment fosters a positive work environment, boosts employee self-esteem, and contributes to a sense of job satisfaction. When employees feel recognized and appreciated, they exhibit higher levels of engagement, commitment, and motivation, which are crucial for the sustained success and vitality of the organization. Recognition, therefore, acts as a catalyst for positive emotional responses, which are instrumental in building a motivated and content workforce.

Employee recognition plays a critical role in reinforcing the behaviors and achievements that propel an organization forward. By celebrating successes and highlighting exemplary conduct, organizations can encourage the replication of these behaviors across the workforce. Recognition serves as a form of feedback, informing employees about the actions and contributions that are valued by the organization. This feedback mechanism helps to align employee efforts with organizational goals, ensuring that everyone is working cohesively towards a shared vision. Furthermore, recognition strengthens the connection between individual performance

175

and organizational success, emphasizing the importance of every employee's contribution to the company's achievements.

Through the strategic use of recognition, organizations can establish benchmarks of excellence that inspire employees to aspire to higher standards of performance. Recognizing outstanding achievements sets a precedent within the organization, defining what excellence looks like and encouraging others to strive for similar accolades. This not only fosters a culture of high performance but also promotes healthy competition among employees, driving them to improve and excel in their roles. Benchmarks for excellence, established through recognition, serve as a guiding light for employees, illuminating the path to success and excellence within the organization.

The practice of employee recognition has a profound impact on organizational culture and performance. A culture that prioritizes and values recognition is characterized by positivity, mutual respect, and collective ambition. In such environments, employees are more likely to take pride in their work, exhibit loyalty to the organization, and go above and beyond in their duties. Recognition also plays a pivotal role in attracting and retaining top talent, as prospective and current employees are drawn to organizations where their efforts are acknowledged and celebrated.

Moreover, the benefits of a recognition-rich culture extend to organizational performance. Engaged and motivated employees are more productive, innovative, and customer-focused, contributing to improved service quality, customer satisfaction, and ultimately, enhanced business outcomes. Recognition, therefore, is not merely a tool for boosting morale but a strategic investment in the organization's human capital and competitive advantage.

Implementing effective employee recognition requires thoughtful consideration and strategic planning. Recognition should be timely, specific, aligned with organizational values, and inclusive of all employees. Organizations should employ a variety of recognition methods to cater to diverse preferences and ensure that acknowledgments are meaningful to the recipients. Furthermore, integrating recognition into the fabric of everyday operations, through both formal programs and informal gestures, can embed appreciation as a core aspect of the organizational culture.

Employee recognition emerges as a critical strategy for enhancing morale, fostering a culture of appreciation, reinforcing positive behaviors, and setting benchmarks for excellence. Its significance transcends the mere acknowledgment of efforts, embodying a powerful motivator that drives employees towards higher achievements and aligns their contributions with organizational goals. By prioritizing recognition, organizations can cultivate a positive work environment, boost employee engagement and satisfaction, and enhance overall performance. Effective recognition, therefore, is not just beneficial—it is essential for nurturing a motivated workforce and achieving organizational success.

Strategies For Effective Recognition

For recognition to resonate and be meaningful, it must be timely, specific, and aligned with the organization's core values. Timeliness ensures that the recognition is directly linked to the achievement, reinforcing the behavior soon after it occurs. Being specific about what is being recognized helps the employee understand the exact behaviors or achievements that are valued, making it more likely they will be repeated. Aligning recognition with the company's values reinforces the importance of these values, embedding them deeper into the corporate culture.

Effective recognition can take many forms, from formal award programs that celebrate outstanding achievements to informal methods such as shout-outs in team meetings, personal notes of thanks, or social media recognition. The key is to ensure that the mode of recognition matches the achievement and resonates with the individual being recognized.

Effective employee recognition is a nuanced strategy that plays a pivotal role in enhancing morale, fostering a positive organizational culture, and encouraging high performance. To be impactful, recognition must be timely, specific, and aligned with the organization's core values. This multifaceted approach ensures that acknowledgment is not only received but is also meaningful and motivational.

The timeliness of recognition is crucial for reinforcing positive behaviors and achievements close to when they occur. Immediate acknowledgment serves as a direct link between the action and the recognition, making the appreciation more relevant and impactful. This promptness ensures that the employee clearly understands which behaviors or accomplishments are being rewarded, enhancing the likelihood of these actions being repeated in the future. Delayed recognition, on the other hand, can diminish its effectiveness, as the connection between the action and the acknowledgment may become blurred over time.

Being specific in recognition involves clearly articulating what exactly is being recognized. This specificity helps employees understand precisely which of their behaviors or achievements are valued by the organization. It eliminates ambiguity, allowing employees to know what actions contribute most positively to their team and the broader organizational goals. Specific acknowledgment not only validates the employee's efforts but also serves as a guide for other team members on the types of contributions that are appreciated and rewarded within the organization.

Recognition that is aligned with the organization's core values serves to reinforce these principles, embedding them more deeply into the corporate culture. When employees are recognized for actions that exemplify the company's values, it

180

underscores the importance of these values in everyday operations and decision-making. This alignment ensures that recognition acts as a tool not just for individual motivation but also for cultivating a values-driven work environment. Employees are encouraged not only to achieve their personal best but also to contribute to the embodiment of organizational values in their daily tasks and interactions.

Effective recognition can manifest in various forms, tailored to match the achievement and resonate with the recipient. The diversity in recognition methods allows organizations to appreciate a wide range of contributions, from significant accomplishments to everyday efforts that drive the company forward.

- Formal Award Programs: These programs are designed to celebrate outstanding achievements through structured awards such as "Employee of the Month" or annual performance awards. Formal recognition often involves ceremonies or events that publicly acknowledge the contributions of individuals or teams, providing a platform for widespread recognition.

- Informal Acknowledgment: Informal methods of recognition, such as shout-outs in team meetings, personal notes of thanks, or social media recognition, offer a flexible and personal way to appreciate employees. These methods can be particularly effective for acknowledging the everyday efforts that contribute to the team's success, fostering a culture of continuous appreciation.

- Peer Recognition: Encouraging peer recognition allows employees to acknowledge and appreciate the contributions of their colleagues. This form of recognition can strengthen team bonds and promote a collaborative work environment. Peer recognition programs can include peer-nominated awards or simple platforms for team members to express gratitude to one another.

Understanding that employees have different preferences for how they receive recognition is key to ensuring that acknowledgment is meaningful and motivating. Tailoring recognition to fit the individual involves considering personal preferences, cultural backgrounds, and the context of the achievement. Some employees may appreciate public acknowledgment, while others may prefer private appreciation. Offering choices in how recognition is received can enhance its impact and ensure that it is valued by the recipient.

Effective employee recognition is a dynamic and strategic process that requires careful consideration of timeliness, specificity, value alignment, and the diversity of recognition methods. By implementing strategies that account for these factors, organizations can ensure that recognition is meaningful, motivational, and aligned with the company's goals and values. Tailoring recognition to fit the individual further enhances its effectiveness, making employees feel genuinely appreciated and motivated to continue contributing positively to the organization. In cultivating a culture of recognition, companies can foster a positive work environment, enhance employee morale, and drive organizational success.

The Role of Empowerment in Employee Engagement

Empowerment is a critical component of a positive corporate culture, essential for fostering engagement,

183

satisfaction, and a sense of ownership among employees. When employees feel empowered, they perceive their work as meaningful and believe they have the autonomy to make decisions that impact their roles and the broader organization. This sense of autonomy and trust from leadership motivates employees to take initiative, innovate, and fully commit to their roles, driving higher levels of performance and job satisfaction.

Empowerment within the corporate realm serves as a cornerstone for cultivating a culture of engagement, satisfaction, and a profound sense of ownership among the workforce. This concept transcends mere delegation, embedding a sense of autonomy, trust, and meaningfulness in employees' roles. When individuals perceive their work as impactful and believe they possess the decision-making authority to influence their environment and the organization at large, a transformative shift occurs. This empowerment fosters a motivational drive among employees, encouraging them to embrace initiative, innovation, and a deep-seated commitment to their roles, which, in turn, enhances performance and job satisfaction.

Empowerment is predicated on the principles of autonomy and trust—key drivers that propel employee motivation. Autonomy grants employees the freedom to approach their tasks and solve problems in ways that they deem most effective, fostering a sense of responsibility and ownership over their work. Trust from leadership, manifested through empowerment, signals confidence in the employees' abilities and decision-making prowess. This combination of autonomy and trust not only validates employees' contributions but also instills a sense of value and respect within them. Consequently, employees are more inclined to invest their full effort and creativity into their work, driven by the knowledge that their actions have a meaningful impact on the organization.

Empowerment is a catalyst for innovation and the taking of initiative within the workplace. When employees feel empowered, they are more likely to explore new ideas, propose innovative solutions, and take proactive steps to address challenges. This entrepreneurial spirit is crucial for organizational growth and adaptability, especially in industries characterized by rapid changes and intense competition. Empowerment encourages a forward-thinking mindset, where employees are not just passive participants but active

185

contributors to the organization's evolution and success. Through fostering an environment where initiative and innovation are celebrated, organizations can tap into the collective creativity and ingenuity of their workforce.

A pivotal aspect of empowerment is fostering a sense of ownership among employees regarding their work and the organization's outcomes. This sense of ownership is deeply motivational, as employees perceive their roles and contributions as integral to the organization's success. Ownership encourages a deeper level of commitment and dedication to quality, as employees view the organization's achievements as a reflection of their personal efforts. Furthermore, when employees feel a sense of ownership, they are more likely to go above and beyond in their roles, displaying increased resilience in the face of challenges and a willingness to invest in long-term outcomes.

Cultivating a culture of empowerment yields numerous benefits for both employees and the organization. For employees, empowerment enhances job satisfaction, reduces job-related stress, and increases engagement and loyalty to the company. These positive outcomes contribute to a more vibrant and productive work environment, where

186

employees are motivated to achieve their best. For the organization, empowerment leads to higher levels of innovation, improved problem-solving, and greater adaptability to market changes. Additionally, a culture of empowerment can serve as a competitive advantage in attracting and retaining top talent, as prospective employees are drawn to workplaces that value and invest in their development and autonomy.

Implementing a culture of empowerment requires intentional strategies and practices. Leaders play a crucial role in this process, needing to communicate trust and confidence in their employees' abilities. This can be achieved through practices such as setting clear expectations, providing resources and support, encouraging participation in decision-making, and offering constructive feedback. Moreover, professional development opportunities and pathways for career progression can further enhance employees' sense of empowerment by equipping them with the skills and knowledge to excel and advance within the organization.

Empowering employees involves more than granting them the freedom to make decisions; it encompasses providing the tools, resources, and support necessary for them to succeed. This can be achieved through several strategies:

- Professional Development Opportunities: Offering training, workshops, and continuing education opportunities enables employees to acquire new skills and knowledge, enhancing their ability to contribute effectively to the organization.
- Autonomy in Task Management: Allowing employees discretion in how they complete their work acknowledges their expertise and judgment, fostering a sense of trust and respect.
- Inclusive Decision-Making: Involving employees in decision-making processes that affect their work or the organization at large demonstrates that their opinions are valued and considered in the strategic direction of the company.
- Feedback Loops: Establishing open channels for feedback encourages employees to share their ideas and suggestions, contributing to continuous improvement and innovation.

The role of empowerment in fostering employee engagement is pivotal. By imbuing employees with autonomy, instilling trust, and encouraging a sense of ownership, organizations can cultivate a motivated, innovative, and committed workforce. The benefits of such a culture extend beyond individual job satisfaction, contributing to the organization's overall performance, adaptability, and competitive standing. Therefore, investing in empowerment strategies is not just beneficial but essential for organizations aiming to thrive in the dynamic and challenging landscape of modern business.

Overcoming Challenges to Recognition and Empowerment

While the benefits of recognition and empowerment are clear, implementing these practices can present challenges, including ensuring consistency, avoiding perceptions of favoritism, and balancing empowerment with accountability. Overcoming these challenges requires clear communication of the criteria for recognition, transparent processes for decision-making, and a commitment to equitable treatment of all employees. Leadership training can also equip managers with the skills to recognize and empower their teams effectively, ensuring that these practices are embedded throughout the organization.

Implementing recognition and empowerment practices within an organization offers a plethora of benefits, including enhanced employee morale, increased productivity, and the fostering of a positive workplace culture. However, the path to successfully integrating these practices is often fraught with challenges. Issues such as maintaining consistency in recognition, circumventing perceptions of favoritism, and striking a balance between empowering employees and ensuring accountability are common stumbling blocks that organizations face. Overcoming these hurdles necessitates a strategic approach, underscored by clear communication, transparent processes, equitable treatment, and targeted leadership training.

One of the primary challenges in the realm of employee recognition is ensuring that recognition efforts are consistent across the organization. Inconsistencies in recognizing employee achievements can lead to diminished morale and a sense of unfairness among the workforce. To address this challenge, organizations must establish clear and uniform criteria for recognition that are directly tied to specific behaviors, achievements, and contributions that align with the organization's goals and values. This standardization ensures that all employees understand what is recognized and valued, thereby fostering a sense of fairness and transparency in the recognition process.

Another significant challenge in implementing recognition and empowerment practices is avoiding perceptions of favoritism. Favoritism, whether real or perceived, can erode trust, reduce employee engagement, and create divisions within the workplace. Combatting this challenge requires a commitment to equitable treatment of all employees. This includes ensuring that recognition and empowerment opportunities are accessible to everyone, regardless of their role, level, or tenure within the organization. Additionally, involving multiple stakeholders in the recognition process can provide diverse perspectives, further mitigating the risk of favoritism.

Empowering employees to take ownership of their work and make decisions is crucial for fostering engagement and innovation. However, this empowerment must be balanced with accountability to ensure that decision-making aligns with organizational goals and standards. Striking this balance involves clearly defining the scope of empowerment, including the boundaries within which employees can make decisions and the expectations for their outcomes. Transparent communication about the rationale behind decisions and the consequences of actions, whether positive or negative, reinforces the link between empowerment and accountability. Implementing transparent processes for both recognition and empowerment decisions is fundamental for overcoming challenges to these practices. Transparency in decision-making processes helps demystify how recognition is awarded and how empowerment opportunities are allocated, contributing to a sense of fairness and inclusivity. This transparency can be achieved through regular communication about the criteria and processes involved in these decisions, as well as providing feedback and explanations for specific recognition and empowerment outcomes.

Equipping managers and leaders with the necessary skills to effectively recognize and empower their teams is essential for embedding these practices throughout the organization. Leadership training programs should focus on developing skills in active listening, unbiased decision-making, effective communication, and feedback delivery. Training leaders to recognize and address their own biases can also help mitigate perceptions of favoritism and ensure equitable treatment of all employees. Furthermore, empowering leaders to model recognition and empowerment behaviors sets a precedent for the entire organization, reinforcing the importance of these practices.

A foundational element in overcoming challenges to recognition and empowerment is a steadfast commitment to the equitable treatment of all employees. This commitment should be reflected in every aspect of the organization's operations, from the criteria used for recognition to the opportunities provided for employee empowerment. Ensuring equity involves regular review and adjustment of practices to address any disparities and maintain alignment with organizational values and goals.

The journey to effectively implement recognition and empowerment practices within an organization is fraught with complexities and challenges. These obstacles, however, are not insurmountable but rather opportunities for strategic refinement and thoughtful application of leadership principles. Key to navigating these challenges is a comprehensive strategy that encompasses consistency in recognition efforts, the mitigation of favoritism perceptions,

193

the harmonious balance between empowerment and accountability, the maintenance of transparency in processes, the provision of leadership training, and a steadfast commitment to equitable treatment across the organization.

A fundamental challenge in recognition practices is ensuring that acknowledgments are consistent and reflective of genuine achievements. Inconsistencies can dilute the impact of recognition and may lead to skepticism regarding its sincerity. Establishing clear criteria for what constitutes recognizable performance and behavior is essential. This clarity helps in standardizing recognition practices, ensuring that all employees understand how and why recognitions are awarded, fostering a culture of meritocracy.

Another pivotal concern is the potential perception of favoritism, which can undermine the integrity of recognition practices. To combat this, organizations must endeavor to make the recognition process as objective and transparent as possible. Utilizing peer recognition programs, where employees have the opportunity to nominate their colleagues for awards, can also help in distributing the responsibility of recognition and reducing biases.

Empowerment, while crucial, must be balanced with accountability to ensure that freedom granted to employees aligns with organizational goals and standards. This balance can be achieved by setting clear expectations from the outset, providing the necessary resources for employees to succeed, and establishing a feedback loop that allows for regular performance discussions. Such measures ensure that empowerment does not devolve into a lack of direction or oversight but is a catalyst for responsible innovation and decision-making.

Transparency in both recognition and empowerment practices is essential for building trust within the organization. Transparent processes ensure that employees understand how decisions are made and how they can influence their own career paths within the company. This openness fosters a sense of fairness and inclusivity, critical components of a positive workplace culture.

Leaders play a crucial role in the successful implementation of recognition and empowerment practices. Providing leadership training that focuses on effective communication, unbiased recognition, and the facilitation of employee empowerment can equip leaders with the tools they need to support their teams effectively. Such training can also help leaders understand the importance of their role in modeling the values and behaviors that define the organizational culture.

Finally, a commitment to equitable treatment is paramount. This commitment involves actively working to ensure that all employees, regardless of their role, level, or background, have access to the same opportunities for recognition and empowerment. Such a commitment reinforces the organization's dedication to fairness and equality, crucial for fostering a sense of belonging and loyalty among the workforce.

While the path to effectively integrating recognition and empowerment into an organization's culture is complex, the strategic adoption of thoughtful approaches can lead to success. By prioritizing consistency, fairness, balance, transparency, leadership development, and equity, organizations can surmount the challenges associated with these practices. The result is a workplace culture that deeply values, motivates, and engages its employees, enhancing both individual and organizational performance. This culture is a critical asset in the modern business landscape, contributing to a resilient and adaptive framework that positions the organization for enduring success amidst ongoing change.

Chapter 8: The Big Picture

Creating a thriving and healthy business culture is a complex yet rewarding endeavor that necessitates a deep-rooted commitment and a consistent, organization-wide effort, with leadership playing a pivotal role. This chapter delves into the multifaceted aspects of cultivating such a culture, highlighting the critical importance of strong leadership, clear and shared values, open communication, meaningful recognition, genuine empowerment, inherent adaptability, and a commitment to continuous learning. In an ever-evolving business landscape, the strategic investment in fostering a positive corporate culture transcends a mere advantageous practice; it emerges as a fundamental necessity for achieving enduring success and ensuring the sustainability of the organization.

At the forefront of establishing a healthy business culture is leadership. Leaders set the tone for the organizational culture through their actions, decisions, and the behaviors they choose to reward. Effective leadership is characterized by authenticity, vision, and the ability to inspire trust and motivate employees towards shared goals. Leaders must embody the values they wish to see throughout the organization, fostering an environment where open communication, innovation, and collaboration are not only encouraged but celebrated.

The foundation of a healthy business culture also rests on the clarity and consistency of its values. These values should accurately reflect the organization's mission and vision, serving as a guiding light for decision-making and behavior at all levels. When values are clearly articulated and deeply ingrained in the organization's practices, they foster a sense of purpose and direction, aligning individual efforts with the collective objectives of the company.

Open communication is another cornerstone of a vibrant corporate culture. It facilitates transparency, trust, and mutual respect among all members of the organization. Cultivating an environment where feedback is freely exchanged, and ideas are openly discussed enables companies to address challenges proactively, leverage diverse perspectives, and foster a sense of inclusion and belonging among employees.

Recognition and empowerment stand as powerful drivers of a positive workplace culture. Acknowledging and rewarding employees' contributions reinforces their value to the organization, boosting morale and encouraging a culture of excellence. Similarly, empowering employees by entrusting them with autonomy and involving them in decision-making processes amplifies their engagement and commitment to the organization's success.

In today's fast-paced and unpredictable business environment, adaptability and continuous learning are essential traits of a healthy business culture. Organizations that embrace change and foster a culture of lifelong learning are better equipped to navigate uncertainties, embrace new opportunities, and stay ahead in a competitive market. This adaptability ensures that the organization remains resilient in the face of change, while a focus on continuous learning keeps the workforce skilled, informed, and motivated.

Investing in a healthy corporate culture is an ongoing journey that requires dedication, strategic vision, and collaborative effort across all levels of the organization. By prioritizing these key elements, companies can cultivate a workplace environment that not only enhances employee satisfaction and well-being but also propels performance, drives innovation, and secures a competitive advantage. In the dynamic context of modern business, the creation and maintenance of such a culture are not merely beneficial; they are imperative for long-term success and organizational sustainability. Through the chapters that follow, we will explore each of these foundational elements in detail, offering insights and strategies for building and sustaining a healthy business culture that thrives amidst the complexities of the contemporary business landscape.

The Role of Strong Leadership

Leadership serves as the foundational pillar upon which the culture of an organization is built. It is the catalyst that shapes behaviors, ethics, and values, steering the company towards its envisioned future. Strong leadership, marked by transparency, integrity, and the ability to inspire, is essential in cultivating a positive organizational culture. This type of leadership not only guides the organization through its present challenges but also lays the groundwork for future success.

The influence of leaders on organizational culture is profound and far-reaching. Leaders set the tone for the entire organization through their actions, decisions, and the behaviors they choose to reward or discourage. By consistently demonstrating transparency and integrity, leaders foster an environment where honesty and ethical conduct are valued and emulated. This commitment to transparency and integrity is crucial for building trust within the organization, as employees look to their leaders for cues on how to behave and what to prioritize.

One of the hallmarks of strong leadership is the ability to inspire and motivate. Leaders who are genuinely committed to the organization's values and possess a clear vision for its future can galvanize their teams to achieve greater heights. They recognize the importance of connecting employees' individual roles to the broader organizational goals, making each team member feel valued and part of something larger than themselves. This sense of purpose is incredibly motivating for employees, driving engagement and fostering a culture where innovation and excellence are pursued.

Trust and respect are the bedrock of a positive organizational culture, and leaders play a pivotal role in cultivating these elements. Leaders who demonstrate a genuine commitment to employee well-being and development earn the respect of their teams. They understand that leadership is not about wielding power but about empowering others to realize their potential. By listening to their employees, valuing their contributions, and providing opportunities for growth, leaders can build a

202

culture of trust and respect. This culture not only enhances employee satisfaction but also encourages open communication, collaboration, and a shared commitment to achieving organizational objectives.

Change is a constant in the business world, and strong leadership is crucial for navigating the organization through these transitions. Leaders who are adept at managing change can guide their organizations through uncertainty with confidence and clarity. They communicate the reasons for change effectively, involve employees in the change process, and provide the support and resources needed to adapt to new circumstances. By leading change proactively and positively, leaders can ensure that the organization not only survives but thrives in the face of new challenges.

Ensuring that the organization remains aligned with its core values and goals is a critical aspect of strong leadership. Leaders must continually reinforce these values and goals, integrating them into the organization's strategies, policies, and practices. This alignment ensures that the organization's actions are consistent with its vision and that employees understand the direction in which the company is headed. Leaders must also be vigilant in identifying and addressing any misalignments that may arise, ensuring that the organization stays true to its values and objectives.

Strong leadership is indispensable for creating and maintaining a healthy organizational culture. Leaders who exemplify transparency, integrity, and the ability to inspire set the foundation for a culture characterized by trust, respect, and a shared sense of purpose. By fostering trust and respect, motivating employees, effectively navigating change, and ensuring alignment with core values and goals, leaders can build a resilient and positive organizational culture. This culture not only enhances employee satisfaction and well-being but also drives performance, innovation, and competitive advantage, underscoring the critical role of strong leadership in achieving long-term organizational success.

Establishing Clear Values

Establishing clear and well-defined values is fundamental to shaping the identity and culture of an organization. These values act as a guiding compass, reflecting the core essence of the company's mission and vision, and setting a clear benchmark for what the organization stands for. When thoughtfully articulated and genuinely integrated, these values influence every decision, policy, and practice within the company, fostering a sense of unity and purpose among its members.

Clear values are the bedrock upon which organizational culture is built. They articulate the company's ethical stance, priorities, and the behaviors it cherishes. By defining what is important, values shape the norms and expectations within the organization, creating a shared language and understanding among employees. This shared understanding is crucial for fostering a cohesive environment where individuals feel a strong sense of belonging and alignment with the organization's objectives.

In the realm of decision-making, values serve as critical criteria that guide choices at both strategic and individual levels. Whether it's deciding on strategic directions, resolving ethical dilemmas, or managing day-to-day operations, values offer a consistent framework for making decisions that are congruent with the organization's core beliefs. This consistency ensures that decisions across the organization reinforce its mission and vision, contributing to a coherent and unified approach to achieving its goals.

The influence of clear values extends to the development of policies and practices within the organization. Policies that are aligned with the organization's values not only ensure compliance with its ethical standards but also reinforce the desired culture. Practices rooted in these values cultivate an environment where positive behaviors are encouraged, and negative behaviors are addressed. This alignment between values, policies, and practices is essential for maintaining integrity and trust within the organization and with its stakeholders.

A company's identity is significantly shaped by its values. These values distinguish the organization from its competitors and define its unique character. When values are clearly defined and genuinely embraced, they strengthen the company's identity, making it more recognizable and appealing to both employees and external stakeholders. This strong identity aids in attracting and retaining talent who share similar values, as well as customers who resonate with the company's ethical stance and priorities.

Perhaps one of the most significant impacts of establishing clear values is their ability to serve as a unifying force within the organization. Values that are shared, celebrated, and lived by everyone in the company rally employees around common goals and principles. This unity fosters a strong sense of community and teamwork, enabling the organization to navigate challenges more effectively and achieve its objectives with a collective effort. The sense of shared purpose that emanates from clear values is a powerful motivator, driving employees to contribute their best towards the success of the organization.

For values to have a lasting impact, they must be genuinely integrated into every aspect of the organization. This integration involves more than just stating values in mission statements or promotional materials; it requires embedding them into the fabric of organizational life. From recruitment and onboarding to performance evaluations and leadership development, values should be a constant reference point that informs actions and decisions. This deep integration ensures that the organization's values are not just words on a page but are lived experiences that shape its culture and identity.

The establishment of clear, well-defined values is crucial for crafting a strong and cohesive organizational culture. These values guide decision-making, influence policies and practices, fortify the company's identity, and serve as a unifying force that rallies employees around shared goals and principles. For values to be effective, they must be genuinely integrated into all facets of the organization, influencing every action and decision. By committing to clear values, organizations can create a positive and resilient culture that not only enhances employee satisfaction and well-being but also drives performance, innovation, and long-term success.

Fostering Open Communication

Fostering open communication within an organization is akin to nurturing the very ecosystem that sustains its vitality and growth. It is the mechanism through which ideas, feedback, and concerns circulate freely, enabling every member of the organization, from leadership to front-line employees, to have their voices heard and valued. This foundational element of a healthy business culture is not only crucial for the smooth operation of daily activities but also pivotal in driving innovation, resolving issues efficiently, and fortifying the sense of community and belonging among employees.

At its core, open communication embodies the principle of transparency and the free exchange of ideas and information. It dismantles barriers to dialogue, making it possible for insights and feedback to flow unimpeded across the organizational hierarchy. This unobstructed flow of communication is essential for ensuring that all members of the organization are aligned with its goals, values, and practices, thereby fostering a cohesive and unified work environment.

Open communication serves as a critical tool in several key areas that underpin organizational health:

- Issue Resolution: By encouraging the sharing of concerns and challenges, open communication facilitates the early identification of issues, allowing for timely intervention and resolution. This proactive approach prevents minor problems from escalating into major crises, safeguarding the organization's operational integrity.

- Innovation and Creativity: A culture of open dialogue stimulates creativity and innovation by providing a platform for the exchange of ideas. When employees feel comfortable sharing their thoughts and suggestions without fear of judgment, the organization benefits from a diverse pool of ideas that can drive improvement and growth.
- Community and Belonging: Open communication fosters a sense of community within the organization. It builds bridges between different levels and departments, nurturing a sense of belonging and mutual respect among employees. This sense of community is crucial for employee satisfaction, engagement, and retention.

Creating an environment that supports open communication requires intentional effort and strategic planning. The following strategies are essential in fostering such an environment:

- Intentional Structures and Practices: Organizations must establish structures and practices that facilitate open dialogue. This can include regular team meetings, open forums, suggestion boxes, and digital platforms designed for sharing ideas and feedback. These structures should be accessible to all employees, ensuring that everyone has the opportunity to contribute to the conversation.

- Leadership Involvement: Leaders play a pivotal role in fostering open communication. By actively engaging in dialogue with employees, soliciting feedback, and sharing information transparently, leaders model the importance of open communication. Their involvement sends a powerful message that communication is valued at the highest levels of the organization.

- Encouraging Transparency and Honesty: Cultivating an environment where transparency and honesty are prioritized is crucial for open communication. This involves creating a safe space where employees can share their thoughts without fear of reprisal. Policies and practices that protect confidentiality and promote ethical behavior reinforce this environment.

- Building Trust: Trust is the foundation upon which open communication is built. Trust is fostered through consistent actions, integrity, and fairness in dealing with all employees. When trust is established, employees are more likely to engage in open communication, sharing their ideas and feedback more freely.

- Training and Development: Providing training and development opportunities for employees and leaders alike in effective communication skills can enhance the quality of dialogue within the organization. Skills such as active listening, empathy, and constructive feedback are essential for nurturing an environment supportive of open communication.

Open communication is indispensable for the creation and maintenance of a healthy business culture. It is the conduit through which ideas flow, issues are addressed, and a sense of community is built. By implementing intentional structures and practices, involving leadership in communication efforts, encouraging transparency and honesty, building trust, and investing in training and development, organizations can foster an environment where open communication thrives. Such an environment not only enhances operational efficiency and innovation but also contributes to building a resilient and positive organizational culture, where every employee feels valued and engaged.

Recognition and Empowerment

Recognition and empowerment within an organization are critical components that contribute significantly to building a positive work environment, enhancing employee morale, and fostering a culture of appreciation and autonomy. When employees are recognized for their contributions in a manner that is timely, specific, and aligned with the organization's core values, it not only validates their efforts but also motivates them and their peers towards sustained excellence. Concurrently, empowerment—granting employees the autonomy to make decisions and take ownership of their work—cultivates a sense of trust between employees and management, encouraging initiative, innovation, and a profound commitment to their roles.

Recognition serves as a powerful tool in acknowledging the hard work and achievements of employees. Effective recognition goes beyond mere acknowledgment; it serves to affirm the value of an employee's contributions to the organization, thereby enhancing their sense of worth and belonging. When recognition is timely, it immediately connects the achievement with the acknowledgment, making the

213

appreciation more impactful. Being specific in recognition ensures that employees understand precisely which actions are being rewarded, encouraging the repetition of such behaviors. Furthermore, aligning recognition with the company's values reinforces these principles as foundational to the organization's success, embedding them deeper into its culture.

Empowerment stands as a testament to the trust an organization places in its employees, granting them the autonomy to steer their work and make decisions. This trust is not given lightly but is a deliberate investment in the capabilities and judgment of the workforce. Empowerment catalyzes a shift in the employee's self-perception, from being mere executors of tasks to being vital contributors to the organization's strategy and success. This shift fosters a deeper engagement with their roles, driving innovation and creativity. Empowered employees are more likely to take initiative, exploring new ideas and approaches with the confidence that they have the support of their leadership.

Creating a culture of appreciation through recognition involves integrating recognition practices into the daily operations of the organization. This can include formal

214

mechanisms, such as award ceremonies and performance bonuses, as well as informal practices, like verbal praise in meetings or personal notes of thanks. The key to fostering a culture of appreciation lies in the consistency of recognition efforts, ensuring that all employees feel seen and valued for their contributions, regardless of their role or level within the organization.

Empowerment cultivates autonomy and trust within the workforce by demonstrating confidence in the employees' abilities to lead projects, solve problems, and make meaningful contributions. This process involves not only granting decision-making authority but also providing the necessary resources, support, and training to succeed. Empowering employees encourages a culture of accountability, where individuals take responsibility for their actions and outcomes, further strengthening the organization's capacity for collective achievement.

The interplay between recognition and empowerment has a synergistic effect on employee morale and job satisfaction. Recognition affirms and celebrates the value of the employees' contributions, while empowerment entrusts them with the autonomy to shape their work and influence

215

the organization's direction. Together, these practices create a dynamic work environment where employees feel appreciated, trusted, and motivated to pursue excellence. This environment not only enhances individual performance but also contributes to the organization's overall productivity and innovation.

Implementing recognition and empowerment effectively requires strategic planning and consistent effort. Organizations can adopt various strategies, such as establishing clear criteria for recognition, creating diverse opportunities for employee empowerment, training managers in effective recognition and empowerment practices, and regularly evaluating the impact of these practices on employee engagement and performance. Additionally, fostering open communication and feedback mechanisms can provide valuable insights into how recognition and empowerment initiatives are perceived by the workforce, enabling continuous improvement.

Recognition and empowerment are indispensable elements of a positive organizational culture, significantly influencing employee morale, engagement, and performance. Through strategic and thoughtful implementation of recognition and empowerment practices, organizations can create an environment where employees feel valued, trusted, and motivated to contribute their best. This not only enhances job satisfaction and performance on an individual level but also drives the organization towards greater innovation, productivity, and success in the competitive business landscape.

Investing in Corporate Culture for Long-term Success

The benefits of nurturing a healthy corporate culture extend far beyond employee satisfaction. Such cultures drive performance, foster innovation, and enhance the organization's competitive advantage. Employees who feel valued, respected, and aligned with their company's values are more engaged, productive, and loyal. This heightened engagement translates into superior customer service, innovative solutions, and an ability to attract and retain top talent. Moreover, a positive corporate culture strengthens the organization's reputation, making it more appealing to customers, investors, and potential employees alike.

217

In the ever-evolving landscape of global business, the significance of a robust and healthy corporate culture cannot be overstated. It is the backbone of an organization, influencing every aspect of its operations, from decision-making processes to employee engagement and customer satisfaction. Investing in corporate culture is an essential strategy for organizations aiming for longevity and sustained success in the competitive market. This investment goes beyond financial resources, encompassing leadership development, effective communication, recognition, continuous learning, empowerment, and strategic change management.

A healthy corporate culture serves as the foundation upon which long-term success is built. It shapes the organization's identity, guiding principles, and operational ethos. Such a culture fosters an environment where innovation thrives, employees are engaged and motivated, and ethical standards are upheld. By investing in the development of a positive culture, organizations can ensure they possess the resilience and adaptability necessary to withstand external pressures and internal challenges.

Leadership plays a pivotal role in shaping and sustaining corporate culture. Investing in leadership development means equipping leaders with the skills and knowledge to effectively inspire, guide, and support their teams. This involves training in areas such as emotional intelligence, effective communication, strategic decision-making, and change management. Leaders who are committed to personal and professional growth can effectively model the values and behaviors that define the corporate culture, influencing their teams to align with these principles.

Effective communication is the lifeblood of a healthy corporate culture. Investing in clear communication channels ensures that information flows freely and transparently throughout the organization. This openness fosters trust among employees, encourages the sharing of ideas and feedback, and facilitates collaborative problem-solving. By prioritizing clear and open communication, organizations can create a culture of inclusivity where every voice is heard and valued.

Recognition is a powerful tool for reinforcing desired behaviors and achievements that align with the organization's goals and values. By implementing comprehensive recognition programs, organizations can acknowledge and reward employees for their contributions, boosting morale and fostering a sense of appreciation. Effective recognition programs are diverse, offering both formal awards and informal acknowledgments, tailored to meet the needs and preferences of the workforce.

A culture that values continuous learning and empowerment encourages employees to take initiative, develop new skills, and contribute to innovation. Investing in professional development opportunities, from workshops and seminars to mentorship programs, demonstrates a commitment to employee growth. Empowering employees to make decisions and take ownership of their work enhances their engagement and commitment to the organization's success.

In a rapidly changing business environment, the ability to manage and adapt to change is crucial for sustainability. Investing in a culture that embraces change involves preparing employees for transitions, involving them in the change process, and supporting them through challenges. A strategic approach to change management ensures that the

220

organization remains agile and responsive to new opportunities and threats.

The rewards of investing in a healthy corporate culture are manifold. Organizations with strong cultures enjoy higher levels of employee engagement, customer satisfaction, and operational efficiency. They are better positioned to attract and retain top talent, foster innovation, and maintain a competitive edge. Moreover, a positive corporate culture contributes to a reputable brand image, attracting customers and partners who share similar values.

A healthy corporate culture is not a static achievement but a living, evolving entity that requires ongoing attention and nurturing. This involves regularly assessing the culture, soliciting feedback from employees, and making adjustments to align with changing goals and market conditions. Organizations must remain committed to the continuous cultivation of their culture, ensuring that it evolves in ways that support long-term success and sustainability.

Investing in corporate culture is indispensable for organizations seeking to thrive in the dynamic and competitive business landscape. By dedicating resources to leadership development, clear communication, recognition, continuous learning, empowerment, and strategic change management, organizations can build resilient and positive cultures. These cultures not only enhance employee satisfaction and operational efficiency but also drive innovation, competitive advantage, and long-term success. Through a concerted effort, commitment at all levels, and a clear vision, organizations can create cultures that are not just enduring but also instrumental in forging a legacy of success and sustainability.

www.ingramcontent.com/pod-product-compliance
Lightning Source LLC
Chambersburg PA
CBHW070854290526
45795CB00001B/116